Data Structures and Analysis of Algorithms in an Easy Way

Dr. Ananthoju Vijay Kumar

Published by

BONFRING®
Intellectual Integrity

ISBN 978-93-92537-42-4

Author

Dr. Ananthoju Vijay Kumar

Bonfring

309, 5th Street Extension, Gandhipuram,

Coimbatore - 641 012,

Tamil Nadu, India.

E-mail: info@bonfring.org

Website: www.bonfring.org

Acknowledgement

It is a great pleasure for me to acknowledge the assistance and support of a large number of individuals who have been responsible for the successful completion of this book titled "Data Structures and Analysis of Algorithms in an Easy Way".

First, I would like to take this opportunity to express my sincere gratitude to Faculty of Engineering & Technology, Jain University, for cooperating me to complete this book in this Institution.

In particular I would like to thank Dr. Hariprasad SA, Director, Faculty of Engineering & Technology, Jain University, for his constant encouragement and expert advice.

It is a matter of immense pleasure to express my sincere thanks to Dr. Geetha madam, Dean, Department of Computer Science and Engineering, Jain University, Bangalore.

Finally, I would like to thank my Guide Dr.T.V. Rajinikanth, Head of the Department, Professor in Computer Science and Engineering, SNIST, Hyderabad.

I am also grateful to family and friends who provided me with every requirement throughout the course.

I would also like to thank one and all who directly or indirectly helped me in completing the book successfully.

TABLE OF CONTENTS

UNIT I

INTRODUCTION TO ALGORITHM DESIGN TECHNIQUES

1. Key Objectives

After completing this unit reader is able to get an idea about algorithm, pseudo code for expressing algorithms, Algorithm performance analysis-Time complexity and Space Complexity, Asymptotic Notations, Substitution method, Master's theorem. Divide and Conquer approach for problem solving, applications-Binary Search, Quick Sort, Merge Sort, Strassen's matrix multiplication.

1.1. Algorithm

We know to solve some problem or to write a program, generally follow some sequence of steps. In simple terms we can define an algorithm as a step by step procedure for problem solving. To show how an algorithm is generally written let us consider the following example.

Algorithm: Add (X, Y, Z)

Step 1: Read the first number

      X<-First Number

Step 2: Read the second number

      Y<- Second Number

Step 3: Add X to Y and Store the result into Z

      Z<-X+Y

Step 4: Stop

1.2. Algorithm Analysis

We generally after writing the algorithm or program need to verify whether it is efficient one or not. To know whether it is efficient or not we perform algorithm analysis. Algorithm analysis is nothing but a study to measuring the time complexity and space complexity. An algorithm is said to be efficient if it runs in minimum time and requires less main memory. Let us try to know what is time complexity and space complexity in nutshell form.

1.2.1. Time Complexity Analysis

A study conducted to calculate the amount of time required running an application or algorithm in the best case, average case and worst case is known as Time Complexity Analysis.

Best case represents the minimum time, average case represents the average time and worst case represents the maximum time required to run an algorithm.

1.2.2. *Space Complexity Analysis*

It is performed to measure the amount of physical memory required to run an algorithm or a program in the best case, average case and worst case.

1.3. Asymptotic Notations

A variety of notations are used to represent the time complexity and space complexity of algorithms, such notations are popularly known as Asymptotic Notations. These are actually mathematical tools to represent the complexity of algorithms or programs. There are several asymptotic notations, out of which here we will try to discuss some very important notations, like Big Oh (O), Omega (Ω) and tita (ω).

1.3.1. *Big Oh (O)*

It is upper bound notation, always used to represent the upper bound time complexity of any algorithm or program.

Def: f (n) = O (g(n)) if there exist some positive constants n, n0 and c such that **f(n)<=c.g(n)** where **n > n0**

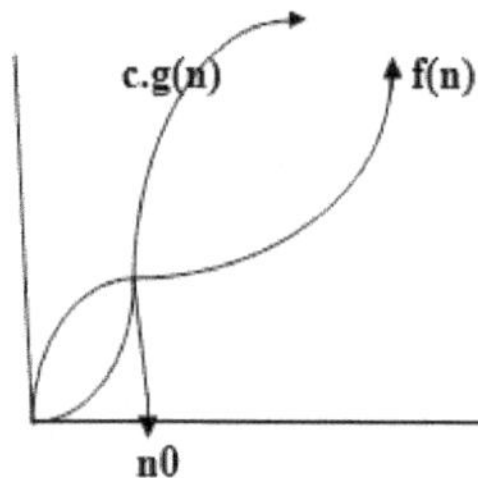

Figure 1.1: Upper Bound Time Complexity

Note: From the diagram it is always clear that f(n) is always less than c.g(n) after n0.

1.3.2. *Omega (Ω)*

It is lower bound notation, always used to represent the lower bound time complexity of any algorithm or program.

Def: f (n) = Ω (g(n)) iff there exist some positive constants n, n0 and c such that **f(n)>=c.g(n)**, where **n>n0**.

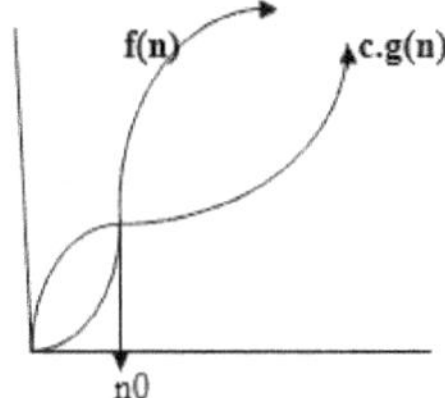

Figure 1.2: Lower Bound Time Complexity

Note: From the diagram it is clear that f(n) is always greater that c.g(n) after n0.

1.3.3. Tita (ω)

It is tight bound notation, always used to represent the average bound time complexity of an algorithm or program.

Def: f(n)= ω(g(n)) iff there exists some positive constants n, n0 and c such that **c1.g(n)<=f(n)<=g(n) where n>n0.**

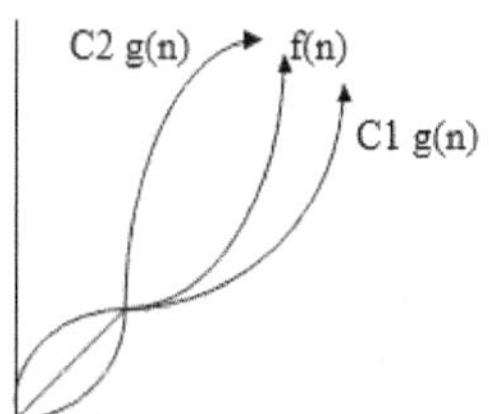

Figure 1.3: Average Bound Time Complexity

Note: Finding an average bound of any algorithm or function is not possible.

There are three methods to solve recurrences. They are substation method, master's method and recurrence tree method.

1.4. Substitution Method

In substation method we blindly assume some solution and then we try to prove it using some mathematical induction.

For example, consider the recurrence $T(n) = 2T(n/2) + n$

We guess the solution as $T(n) = O(nLogn)$. Now we use induction to prove our guess.

We need to prove that T(n) <= cnLogn. We can assume that it is true for values smaller than n.

$$T(n) = 2T(n/2) + n$$
$$<= cn/2Log(n/2) + n$$
$$= cnLogn - cnLog2 + n$$
$$= cnLogn - cn + n$$
$$<= cnLogn$$

1.5.   Recurrence Tree Method

In this method, we draw a recurrence tree and calculate the time taken by every level of tree. Finally, we sum the work done at all levels. To draw the recurrence tree, we start from the given recurrence and keep drawing till we find a pattern among levels. The pattern is typically a arithmetic or geometric series.

For example, consider the recurrence relation.

$$T(n) = T(n/4) + T(n/2) + cn2$$

$$cn^2$$
$$/ \quad \backslash$$
$$T(n/4) \quad T(n/2)$$

If we further break down the expression T(n/4) and T(n/2), we get following recursion tree.

$$cn^2$$
$$/ \qquad \backslash$$
$$c(n^2)/16 \quad c(n^2)/4$$
$$/ \ \backslash \qquad / \ \backslash$$
$$T(n/16) \quad T(n/8) \ T(n/8) \quad T(n/4)$$

Breaking down further gives us following.

$$cn^2$$
$$/ \qquad \backslash$$
$$c(n^2)/16 \qquad c(n^2)/4$$
$$/ \ \backslash \qquad / \ \backslash$$
$$c(n^2)/256 \quad c(n^2)/64 \ c(n^2)/64 \quad c(n^2)/16$$
$$/ \ \backslash \ / \ \backslash \ / \ \backslash \quad / \ \backslash$$

To know the value of T(n), we need to calculate sum of tree nodes level by level. If we sum the above tree level by level, we get the following series.

T(n) = c (n^2 + 5(n^2)/16 + 25(n^2)/256) + ...

The above series is geometrical progression with ratio 5/16.

To get an upper bound, we can sum the infinite series.

We get the sum as (n2) / (1 - 5/16) which is O (n2).

1.6.   Master's Theorem

Master Method is a direct way to get the solution. The master method works only for following type of recurrences or for recurrences that can be transformed to following type.

T(n) = aT(n/b) + f(n) where a >= 1 and b > 1

There are following three cases:

1. If $f(n) = \Theta(n^c)$ where $c < Log_b a$ then $T(n) = \Theta(n^{Log_b a})$
2. If $f(n) = \Theta(n^c)$ where $c = Log_b a$ then $T(n) = \Theta(n^c Log\, n)$
3. If $f(n) = \Theta(n^c)$ where $c > Log_b a$ then $T(n) = \Theta(f(n))$

Master method is mainly derived from recurrence tree method. If we draw recurrence tree of T(n) = aT(n/b) + f(n), we can see that the work done at root is f(n) and work done at all leaves is $\Theta(n^c)$ where c is $Log_b a$ and the height of recurrence tree is $Log_b n$.

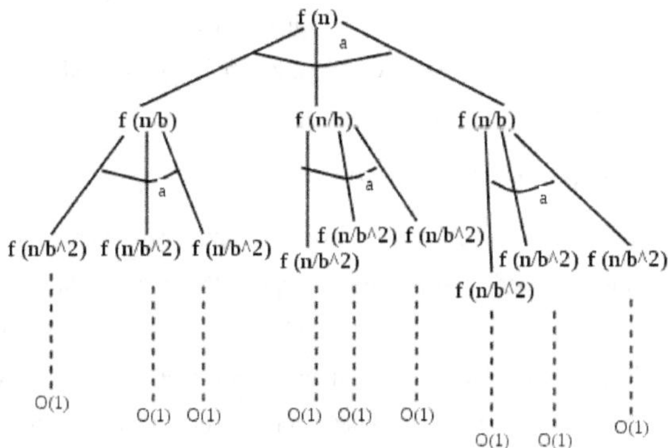

Figure 1.4: Recurrence Tree Method

In recurrence tree method, we calculate total work done. If the work done at leaves is polynomial more, then leaves are the dominant part, and our result becomes the work done at leaves (Case 1). If work done at leaves and root is asymptotically same, then our result becomes height multiplied by work done at any level (Case 2). If work done at root is asymptotically more, then our result becomes work done at root (Case 3).

Examples of Some Standard Algorithms Whose Time Complexity Can be Evaluated Using Master Method

1. **Merge Sort:** $T(n) = 2T(n/2) + \Theta(n)$. It falls in case 2 as c is 1 and $Log_b a]$ is also 1. So, the solution is $\Theta(n \; Logn)$.
2. **Binary Search:** $T(n) = T(n/2) + \Theta(1)$. It also falls in case 2 as c is 0 and $Log_b a$ is also 0. So, the solution is $\Theta(Logn)$.

1.7. Algorithm Design Techniques

To solve some problem, we adapt different techniques or approaches known as problem solving techniques. Generally, after finding some solution to any problem we try to convert that solution into algorithm. To write these algorithms we have several techniques known as algorithm design techniques or algorithm writing techniques.

Algorithm design techniques are basically divided into four types, they are:

1. Divide and conquer
2. Greedy method
3. Back tracking
4. Dynamic programming

Each of these techniques have their own importance, for example divide and conquer technique is best suitable for sorting and searching, greedy approach and dynamic programming techniques are suitable for optimization problems.

1.7.1. *Divide and Conquer Technique*

Divide and conquer technique is used to solve very complex problems and conceptually very difficult problems. In the divide and conquer technique the given problem is divided into sub problems and these sub problems are also divided into sub problem in this manner a problem is divided until we get some solvable problem. In the next step solution of these sub problems are merged to find the solution to the actual given problem. Divide and conquer technique can be used to find solution to the searching, sorting and optimization problems. The two most efficient sorting technique like quick sort and merge sort are good examples of divide and conquer technique. Let us try to learn about these sorting techniques one by one.

1.7.2. *Quick Sort Technique*

Quick sort is an efficient sorting technique compared with merge sort and other sorting techniques. Quick sort follows divide and conquer technique for problem solving. This recursive technique is proposed by Tony Hoare. In quick sort to sort the given n numbers, one is picked as the pivot, the elements which are less than the pivot are placed on the left side to the pivot and greater elements are placed on the right side of the pivot. We can select any element as the pivot. Generally, we pick the first, last or the middle.

Ex: 10,80,30,90,40,50,70

Let us choose 70 as the pivot

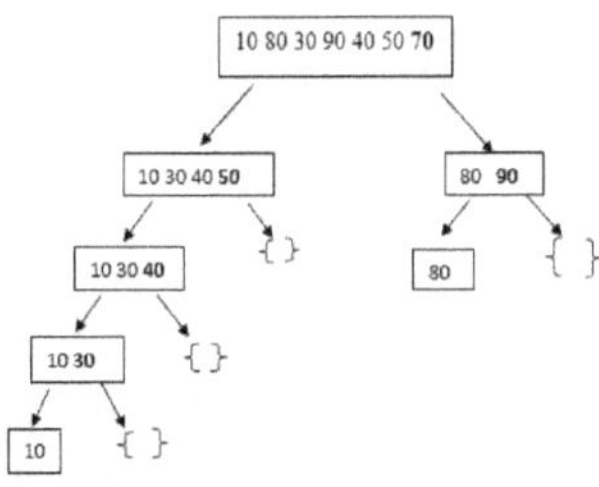

Figure 1.5: Quick Sort Demo

Pseudo code for quick sort

```
QuickSort (int arr[], int low, int high)
{
   if(low<high)
     {
           Pi=partition(arr,low,high)
              QuickSort(arr,low,pi-1);
              QuickSort(arr,pi+1,high)

     }
   }
```

Pseudo code for Partition algorithm

```
Partition (int arr [], int low, int high)
  {
i=low-1;
pivot=arr[high];
for (j=low;j <=high-1; j++)
  {
      if(a[i]<=pivot)
```

        {

        I++;

        swap arr[i] and arr[j];

        }

        }

        swap arr[i+1] and arr[high];

        return(i+1);

        }

Time Complexity: Average and Best Performance is O(nlogn)

Worst Case is O(n*n)

Merge Sort Technique

Like Quick Sort, Merge Sort is also a divide and conquer technique-based algorithm. It is proposed by John Von Neuman in 1945. Merge Sort algorithm divides the given array of elements into two sub arrays of equal size. Again, the two sub arrays are also divided into two of the equal size until we get a sub array with a single element. In the next step these sorted sub arrays are merged. Merge sort time complexity is O(nlogn) in all the 3 (best, average and worst) cases.

Example: Sort the following array of elements using merge sort.

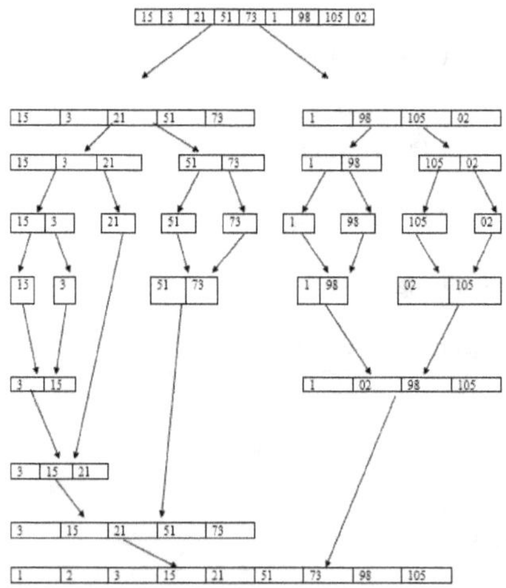

Figure 1.6: Merge Sort Example

Algorithm: Merge Sort (int a [], int l, int r)

Step 1: Check whether the no of elements in the array are more than 1 or not

   If(r>l)

Step 2: Calculate the middle point m=(l+r)/2

Step 3: Call the merge sort function to sort the left sub array

   Mergesort (a, l, m)

Step 4: Call the merge sort function to sort the right sub array

   Mergesort (a, m+1, r)

Step 5: Call the merge function to merge the all sublists

   Merge (a, l, m. r)

Pseudo Code for Merge Function

```
Merge(int a[], int l, int m, int l)

{
    int i,j,k;
    int n1=m-l+1;
    int n2=r-m;
// copy elements of left sub array into L[]
for(i=0;i<=n1;i++)
        L[i]=a[l+i];
//copy elements of right sub array into R[]
for (j=0;j<=n2; j++)
  R[j]=a[m+j+1];
i=0;j=0; k=0;


while(i<n1 && j<n2)
{
    if(L[i]<=R[j])
      {
          a[k]=L[i];
          i++;k++;
```

```
        }
    else
        {
            A[k]=R[j];
            j++;k++;
        }
    //copy the remaining elements of L [] into a []
    while(i<n1)
      {
          a[k]=L[i];
          i++;k++;
      }
    // copy the remaining elements of R[] into a[]
    while(j<n2)
      {
          A[k]=R[j];
          j++;k++;
      }  }
```

1.8.   Strassen's Matrix Multiplication Algorithm

Strassen's has proposed an algorithm for multiplication of two 2*2 matrices which requires only 7 recursive calls. So, using Strassen's approach we can reduce the time complexity.

The general approach for matrix multiplication based on divide and conquers approach is as follows.

$$\begin{bmatrix} a & b \\ c & d \end{bmatrix} \begin{bmatrix} e & f \\ g & h \end{bmatrix} = \begin{bmatrix} ae+bg & af+bh \\ ce+dg & cf+dh \end{bmatrix}$$

In divide and conquer technique to multiply two 2*2 matrices we will divide the matrix into 4 1*1 matrices and we use the general procedure for the matrix multiplication.

In strassens matrix multiplication approach we use the following procedure for matrix multiplication.

$$\begin{bmatrix} a & b \\ c & d \end{bmatrix} \begin{bmatrix} e & f \\ g & h \end{bmatrix} = \begin{bmatrix} p5+p4-p2+p6 & p1+p2 \\ p3+p4 & p1+p5-p3-p7 \end{bmatrix}$$

p1=a(f-h), p2=(a+b)h, p3=(c+d)e, p4=d(g-e)

p5=(a+d)(e+h), p6=(b-d)(g+h), p7=(a-c)(e+f)

Strassen's matrix multiplication requires only 7 recursions whereas naïve method and simple divide and conquer approach needs 8 recursions.

Time Complexity: T (N) = 7T (N/2) + O (N*N)

Generally, we use some other algorithms for matrix multiplication because of some reasons like so many constants are used in Strassen's algorithm and too many errors.

Important Short Answer Questions

1. Define Data Structure
2. Define Algorithm
3. What is pseudo code?
4. What is algorithm analysis?
5. What is time complexity analysis?
6. What is space complexity analysis?
7. Explain about asymptotic notations.
8. Write a short note on substitution method.
9. What is worst case time complexity?
10. What is best case time complexity?
11. What is average case time complexity?
12. Write a short note on Strassen's matrix multiplication.

Important Long Answer Questions

1. Write an algorithm and pseudo code for multiplication of two numbers. Also discuss about time complexity and space complexity of your algorithm.
2. Explain about the divide and conquer technique with some example.

3. Write in brief about quick sort technique using an example. Also write algorithm for quick sort.

4. Write in brief about binary search technique using an example. Also write algorithm for binary search.

5. Write in brief about merge sort technique using an example. Also write an algorithm for merge sort.

6. Write a C++ program for quick sort.

7. Write a C++ program for binary search.

8. Write a C++ program for merge sort.

UNIT II

GREEDY APPROACH TO PROBLEM SOLVING

2. Key Objectives

In this unit we are going to learn about disjoint sets, union and find algorithm, Greedy Method and its applications. Heaps, operations on heaps, heap representation, priority queues and operations on priority queue.

2.1. Disjoint Set Data Structure

Disjoint set data structure keeps track of set of elements, which are divided into a no of disjoint subsets. It is also known as union and find algorithm and merge find set algorithm. This algorithm is proposed by Bernard A Gallel and Michael J. Fischer in 1964.

1. Disjoint set data structure plays a vital role in Kruskal's algorithm to find the MCST.
2. It is used to find, whether a vertex is a member of graph or not.
3. Whether there is a cycle in the undirected graph or not and etc.

2.2. Job Sequencing with Dead Lines

In Job sequencing with deadlines problem we will be given n no of jobs. Where, each job is associated with some profit and time. If we can complete the jobs in the given time bound then only we get the profit associated with that job otherwise we get zero profit. In this problem our major duty is to prepare a job schedule which gives us the maximum profit. Here we won't bother how many jobs are completed successfully. While preparing this job schedule we should assume that each job takes the equal amount of time and at a time we can't perform more than one job.

Ex:

Job Id	Dead Line	Profit
A	4	20
B	1	10
C	1	40
D	1	30

In the above problem we pick job C first because it gives us the maximum profit and after completion of the job c we pick job A because we can't process the jobs B and C as their dead line reached. By processing jobs C and A, we get profit 60.

The Simple way to solve job sequencing problem with deadlines is as follows:

Step 1: Arrange all the jobs in the descending order of their profit.

Step 2: Pick the job from first to last, if it is feasible to complete that job other wise move to the next job.

Algorithm for Job Sequencing with Deadline

Step 1: Sort the jobs in the descending order of their profit.

Step 2: Pick the first job and add it to the result sequence set.

Step 3: Do the following for the n-1 jobs.

(a) If the current job can fit in the result sequence without missing the deadline, add the current job to the result set otherwise ignore the current job.

Time complexity for the above solution is O (n*n) which can be optimized using disjoint set data structure.

//Program to find the maximum profit job sequence, from the given array of jobs with deadlines and profits.

```cpp
#include<iostream.h>
#include<algorithm.h>
// structure to represent a job
Struct job
{
  char id;
int dead, profit;
};
// function to compare the profit of two jobs
bool comparison(job a, job b)
{
   return(a.profit>b.profit)
}
// return the maximum no of plot forms required
void printJobScheduling (Job arr[], int n)
   {
```

```cpp
    // sort all jobs according to decreasing order of their profit.
sort (arr,arr+n, comparison)
  int result[n];  // to store result sequence
bool slot[n]; // to keep track of free slot
// initialize all slots to be free
for(int i=0; i<n;i++)

slot[i]=false;

// iterate through all jobs

For(int i=0;i<n;i++)

 {// we will allot the last slot to the job

    for (int j=min(n, arr[i], dead)-1; j>=0; j--)

      {

          if(slot[j]==false)  // free slot

    {    result[j]=I; // add this job to result

         slot[j]=true;

            break;

        }

}

}

// print the result

for(int i=0;i<n;i++)

   if(slot[i])

      cout<<arr[result[i]].id<<" ";

}

// end of print jobscheduling

void main()

  {

      job arr[] = {{'a', 2, 100}, {'b', 1, 19}, {'c', 2, 24}. {'d', 1, 25}, {'e', 3, 15}};

      cout<<"following is the maximum profit sequence";

      printJobScheduling(arr,5);

}
```

2.3. Kruskal's Algorithm

Kruskal's algorithm is a greedy method-based technique most commonly used to find the minimum cost spanning tree. If the given graph is only with the few edges then kursukal's algorithm is the most suitable algorithm. If the given graph is with the too many edges (up to n*n) then greedy method is efficient.

Performance Comparison:

Prim's algorithm performance is O (n*n)

Kruskal's algorithm performance is O (logn)

Algorithm:

Step 1: Remove parallel edges and loops of the given graph.

Step 2: Arrange all the edges in the ascending order of their Weight.

Step 3: Pick an edge with the minimum cost/weight and add this edge with the spanning tree if it.

Wouldn't create a cycle?

Step 4: Repeat step3 until all vertices are covered.

Ex:

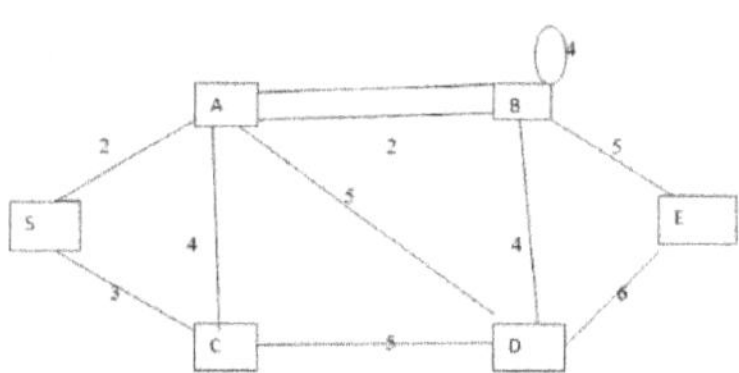

Figure 2.1: Graph G

Consider the above graph and find the minimum cost spanning tree for it.

Step 1: Since there are loops and parallel edges in the graph remove them.

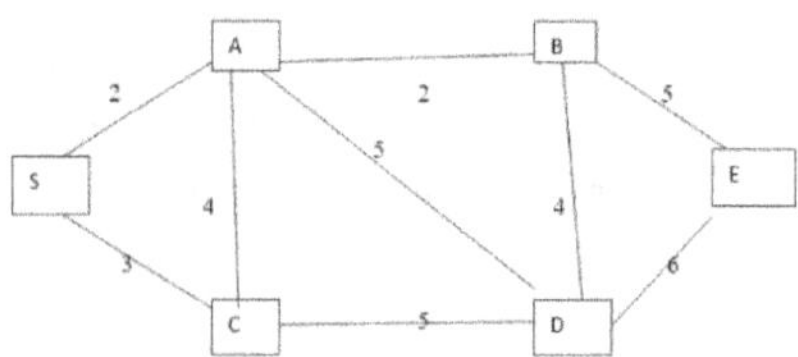

Figure 2.2: Graph G After Removing Self Loops and Parallel Edges

Step 2: The following table shows edges along with weights in ascending order.

Edges	Weights
(A, S)	2
(A, B)	2
C, S)	3
(A, C)	4
(B, D)	4
(C, D)	5
(B, E)	5
(D, E)	6

Step 3: Minimum Cost Spanning Tree.

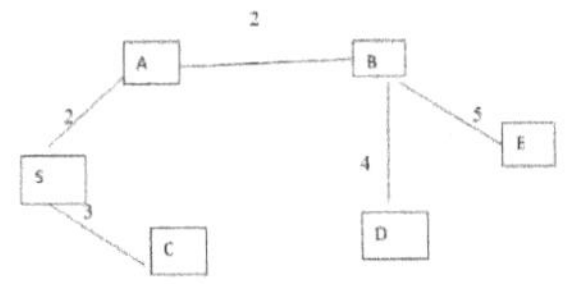

Figure 2.3: Minimum Cost Spanning Tree T

1. #include <stdio.h>

2. #include <stdlib.h>

3. #include <string.h>

4. #include <iostream>

5.

6. using namespace std;

7.

8. // a structure to represent a weighted edge in graph

9. struct Edge

10. {

11.　　int src, dest, weight;

12. };

13.

14. // a structure to represent a connected, undirected and weighted graph

15. struct Graph

16. {

17.　　// V-> Number of vertices, E-> Number of edges

18.　　int V, E;

19.

20.　　// graph is represented as an array of edges. Since the graph is

```
21.      // undirected, the edge from src to dest is also edge from dest
22.      // to src. Both are counted as 1 edge here.
23.      struct Edge* edge;
24. };
25.
26. // Creates a graph with V vertices and E edges
27. struct Graph* createGraph(int V, int E)
28. {
29.    struct Graph* graph = (struct Graph*) malloc(size of(struct Graph));
30.    graph->V = V;
31.    graph->E = E;
32.
33.    graph->edge = (struct Edge*) malloc(graph->E * sizeof(struct Edge));
34.
35.    return graph;
36. }
37.
38. // A structure to represent a subset for union-find
39. struct subset
40. {
41.      int parent;
42.      int rank;
43. };
44.
45. // A utility function to find set of an element i
46. // (uses path compression technique)
47. int find(struct subset subsets[], int i)
48. {
49.    // find root and make root as parent of i (path compression)
50.    if (subsets[i]. parent! = i)
51.      subsets[i]. parent = find(subsets, subsets[i].parent);
52.
53.    return subsets[i]. parent;
54. }
```

```
55.
56.  // A function that does union of two sets of x and y
57.  // (uses union by rank)
58.  void Union (struct subset subsets [], int x, int y)
59.  {
60.     int xroot = find (subsets, x);
61.     int yroot = find (subsets, y);
62.
63.     // Attach smaller rank tree under root of high rank tree
64.     // (Union by Rank)
65.     if (subsets[xroot]. rank < subsets[yroot].rank)
66.        subsets[xroot]. parent = yroot;
67.     else if (subsets[xroot]. rank > subsets[yroot].rank)
68.        subsets[yroot]. parent = xroot;
69.
70.     // If ranks are same, then make one as root and increment
71.     // its rank by one
72.     else
73.     {
74.        subsets[yroot]. parent = xroot;
75.        subsets[xroot]. rank++;
76.     }
77.  }
78.
79.  // Compare two edges according to their weights.
80.  // Used in qsort () for sorting an array of edges
81.  int myComp(const void* a, const void* b)
82.  {
83.     struct Edge* a1 = (struct Edge*) a;
84.     struct Edge* b1 = (struct Edge*) b;
85.     return a1->weight > b1->weight;
86.  }
87.
88.  // The main function to construct MST using Kruskal's algorithm
```

```
89.  void KruskalMST (struct Graph* graph)
90.  {
91.     int V = graph->V;
92.     struct Edge result[V]; // Tnis will store the resultant MST
93.     int e = 0; // An index variable, used for result[]
94.     int i = 0; // An index variable, used for sorted edges
95.
96.     // Step 1:  Sort all the edges in non-decreasing order of their weight
97.     // If we are not allowed to change the given graph, we can create a copy of
98.     // array of edges
99.     qsort(graph->edge, graph->E, size of (graph->edge [0]), myComp);
100.
101.            // Allocate memory for creating V ssubsets
102.            struct subset *subsets = (struct subset*) malloc(V * sizeof(struct
       subset));
103.
104.            // Create V subsets with single elements
105.            for (int v = 0; v < V; ++v)
106.            {
107.               subsets[v]. parent = v;
108.               subsets[v]. rank = 0;
109.            }
110.
111.            // Number of edges to be taken is equal to V-1
112.            while (e < V - 1)
113.            {
114.                // Step 2: Pick the smallest edge. And increment the index
115.                // for next iteration
116.                struct Edge next_edge = graph->edge[i++];
117.
118.                int x = find (subsets, next_edge.src);
119.                int y = find (subsets, next_edge. dest);
120.
121.                // If including this edge does't cause cycle, include it
```

```cpp
122.            // in result and increment the index of result for next edge
123.            if (x ! = y)
124.            {
125.                result[e++] = next_edge;
126.                Union(subsets, x, y);
127.            }
128.            // Else discard the next_edge
129.        }

131.        // print the contents of result [] to display the built MST
132.        cout<<"Following are the edges in the constructed MST\n";
133.        for (i = 0; i < e; ++i)
134.            print f ("%d -- %d == %d\n", result[i].src, result[i]. dest,
135.                result[i]. weight);
136.        return;
137.    }

139.    // Driver program to test above functions
140.    int main()
141.    {
142.        /* Let us create following weighted graph
143.            10
144.        0--------1
145.        /\    /
146.    6/    \5 /15
147.    /    \/
148.    2--------3
149.    4    */
150.        int V = 4; // Number of vertices in graph
151.        int E = 5; // Number of edges in graph
152.        struct Graph* graph = create Graph (V, E);

154.        // add edge 0-1
155.        graph->edge[0].src = 0;
```

```c
156.            graph->edge[0]. dest = 1;
157.            graph->edge[0]. weight = 10;
158.
159.            // add edge 0-2
160.            graph->edge[1].src = 0;
161.            graph->edge[1]. dest = 2;
162.            graph->edge[1]. weight = 6;
163.
164.            // add edge 0-3
165.            graph->edge[2].src = 0;
166.            graph->edge[2]. dest = 3;
167.            graph->edge[2]. weight = 5;
168.
169.            // add edge 1-3
170.            graph->edge[3].src = 1;
171.            graph->edge[3]. dest = 3;
172.            graph->edge[3]. weight = 15;
173.
174.            // add edge 2-3
175.            graph->edge[4].src = 2;
176.            graph->edge[4]. dest = 3;
177.            graph->edge[4]. weight = 4;
178.
179.            Kruskal MST (graph);
180.
181.            return 0;
182.        }
```

Output:

Following are the edges in the constructed MCST.

2 - - 3 = 4

0 - - 3 = 5

0 - - 1 = 10

2.4.   0/1 Knap Sack Problem

0/1 knap Sack problem is a maximization problem or optimization problem. In 0/1 knapsack problem we will be given n no of objects where each object will be associated with some weight and profit. We are requested to arrange these objects into knapsack to get the maximum profit. The 0/1 knapsack problem can be solved using greedy method, dynamic programming and back tracking problem.

Greedy Method: Let us assume there are n objects and each object is associated with some profit pi and weight wi. Assume knapsack capacity is m.

$$\sum_{I=1}^{n1} Wi <= m \text{ where } n1 <= n$$

So in the greedy approach every time we pick some maximum profit giving object to place in the knapsack if possible.

Note: KnapSack capacity is 15.

Objects	O1	O2	O3	O4	O5
Profits	10	5	15	8	4
Weight	10	2	3	4	4
P/W	1	2.5	5	2	1

Example: To pick the object that we wants to insert into the knapsack we consider the profit/weight factor, in the above problem object o3 is maximum profit giving object so, we insert object o3 first into knapsack. After that we pick o2 to insert, then o4. After o3, o2 and o4 objects are inserted, after insertion of o3, o2 and o4 the remaining knapsack capacity is 6. At this time we can't insert object o1 into the knapsack because its weight is 10 which is more than the remaining storage capacity of the knapsack, so we inset object o5. By doing this profit we get is 32.

```
/* A Naive recursive implementation of 0-1 Knapsack problem */
#include<stdio.h>
// A utility function that returns maximum of two integers
int max (int a, int b) {return (a > b)? a: b;}
// Returns the maximum value that can be put in a knapsack of capacity W
int knapsack(int W, int wt[], int val[], int n)
{
```

```c
// Base Case
if (n == 0 || W == 0)
    return 0;
// If weight of the nth item is more than Knapsack capacity W, then
// this item cannot be included in the optimal solution
if (wt[n-1] > W)
    return knapsack (W, wt, val, n-1);
// Return the maximum of two cases:
// (1) nth item included
// (2) not included
else return max(val[n-1] + knapsack (W-wt[n-1], wt, val, n-1),
        knapSack(W, wt, val, n-1)
        );
}
// Driver program to test above function
int main()
{
    int val [] = {10,5,15,8,4};
    int wt [] = {10, 2,3,4,4};
    int W = 15;
    int n = sizeof(val)/size of (val [0]);
    print f ("%d", knapSack (W, wt, val, n));
    return 0;
}
```

2.5. Single Source Shortest Path Problem

Single source shortest path problem is all about finding the shortest path from one vertex to the remaining all other vertices. Single source shortest path problem is a minimization problem to solve this problem we can use greedy method or dynamic programming. Most popular greedy algorithm to find a solution to the single source shortest path problem is Dijkstra algorithm. Dijkstra algorithm can be used on weighted directed graphs and unweighted directed graphs. To understand about the dijkstra algorithm let us consider some problem.

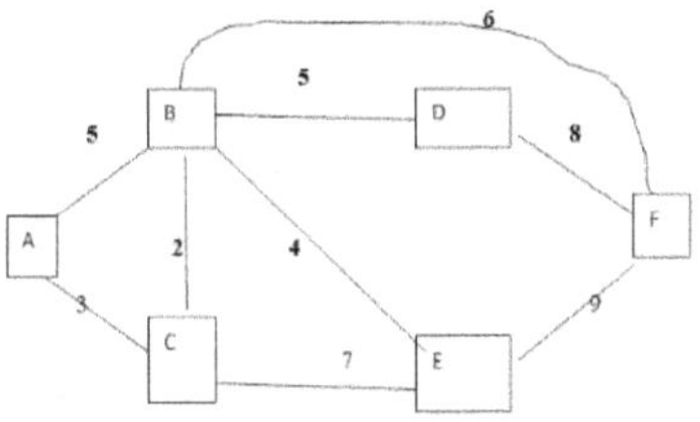

Figure 2.4: Graph H1

Sol: Let us try to find the shortest path from vertex A to remaining all other vertices using Dijkstra algorithm. First pick the vertex A as the starting vertex, from A we have direct path to B and C. Update the keys of B and C as 5 and 3, and weight/key for the remaining vertices will be ∞.

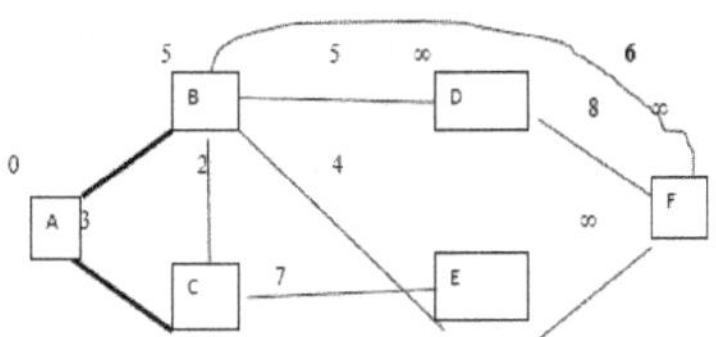

Figure 2.5: Graph H2

Now let us try to find the shortest path to the remaining vertices via B and C. At this point we try to find the shortest path from vertex C first because it is the vertex with the minimum key i.e. 3. So now we should try to find the all vertices which are directly connected from vertex C. From vertex C actually, A, B and E are directly connected. Whereas A is starting point so ignore A, remaining vertices are B and E. If we consider a path from A to B via C, cost will be 5, which is not less than key value of B, it is of no use. Whereas the path cost of A-E is 10, which is less than the key value of E (key value of E is ∞). So update the key value of E to 10.

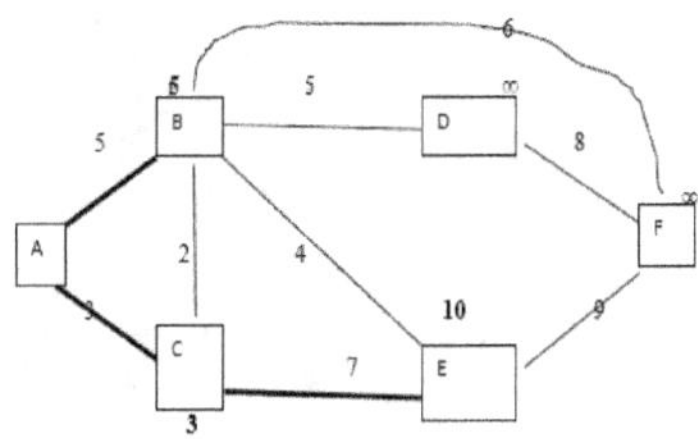

Figure 2.6: Graph H3

To find the shortest path to the remaining uncovered vertices we need to choose the next vertex with the minimum key. Next minimum key vertex is B, so from B we should consider all the vertices which are adjacent to B and which are not included in the shortest path so far. For B, vertices D, E and F are adjacent, so we can find the shortest path to these vertices from A, via B. Path cost of A to D via B is 10, which is less than key value of D (∞), so we update the key value of D as 10. Similarly, the path cost of A to F via B is 11, which is less than the key value of F, so we update the key value of F as 11. The path cost of A to E via B is 9 which is less than the key value of E, so we update the key value of E as 9 and ignore the path via C. The latest shortest path from A we can see in the following diagram.

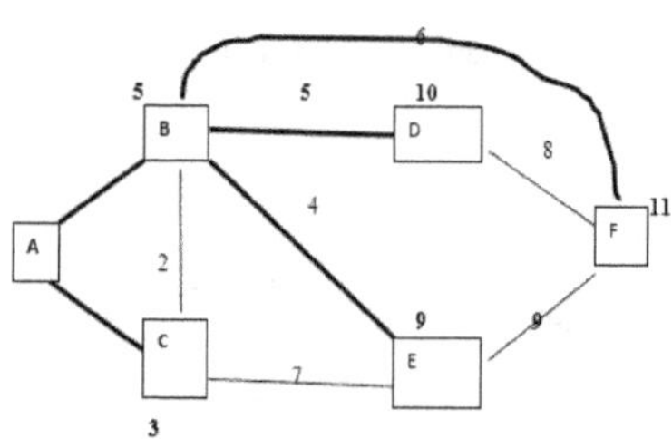

Figure 2.7: Graph H4

Next vertex with the minimum key is E which is 9, so we need to proceed further from E. For E vertex there is only one adjacent vertex that is F. If we consider the path from A to F via E, cost of the path will be 18 which is not less than the key value of F, So it is of no use. In the next step we pick the vertex D because it is the next minimum weight. For vertex D there is only one adjacent vertex i.e., F. If we consider the path from A to F via B and D the cost of the path will be 18 which is not less than the key value of F, so ignore it. After D, the next minimum key vertex is F, for F there are no adjacent vertices so we stop here. The following graph will show as the shortest path of the given graph from vertex A to all the remaining vertices.

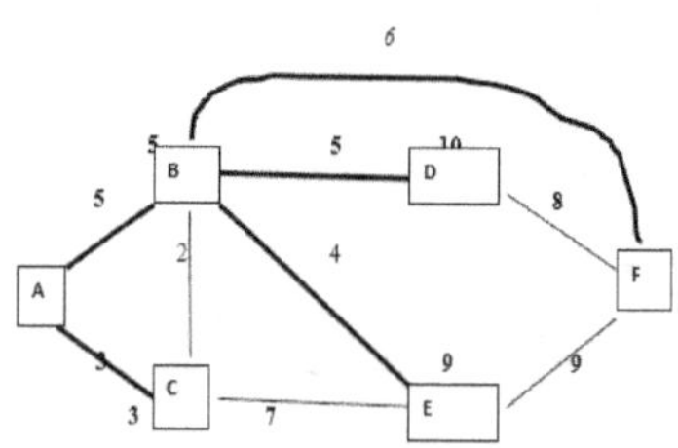

Figure 2.8: Graph H5

Table 2.1: Shortest Path from Vertex A to Remaining All Vertices

Source	Destination	Shortest Path	Cost
A	B	A-B	5
	C	A-C	5
	D	A-B-D	10
	E	A-B-E	9
	F	A-B-F	11

```c
#include <stdio.h>

#include <limits.h>
  // Number of vertices in the graph
#define V 6
  // A utility function to find the vertex with minimum distance value, from
// the set of vertices not yet included in shortest path tree
int min Distance (int dist[], bool sptSet[])
{
  // Initialize min value
  int min = INT_MAX, min_index;
   for (int v = 0; v < V; v++)
    if (sptSet[v] == false && dist[v] <= min)
      min = dist[v], min_index = v;
    return min_index;
}
  // A utility function to print the constructed distance array
int printSolution(int dist[], int n)
{
  print f("Vertex   Distance from Source\n");
  for (int i = 0; i < V; i++)
    printf("%d tt %d\n", i, dist[i]);
}
  // Function that implements Dijkstra's single source shortest path algorithm
// for a graph represented using adjacency matrix representation
void dijkstra(int graph[V][V], int src)
{
   int dist[V]; // The output array.  dist[i] will hold the shortest
```

```c
        // distance from src to i
    bool sptSet[V]; // sptSet[i] will be true if vertex i is included in shortest
            // path tree or shortest distance from src to i is finalized
    // Initialize all distances as INFINITE and stpSet[] as false
    for (int i = 0; i < V; i++)
        dist[i] = INT_MAX, sptSet[i] = false;
        // Distance of source vertex from itself is always 0
    dist[src] = 0;
        // Find shortest path for all vertices
    for (int count = 0; count < V-1; count++)
    {
        // Pick the minimum distance vertex from the set of vertices not
        // yet processed. u is always equal to src in the first iteration.
        int u = minDistance(dist, sptSet);
        // Mark the picked vertex as processed
        sptSet[u] = true;
        // Update dist value of the adjacent vertices of the picked vertex.
        for (int v = 0; v < V; v++)
            // Update dist[v] only if is not in sptSet, there is an edge from
            // u to v, and total weight of path from src to v through u is
            // smaller than current value of dist[v]
            if (! sptSet[v] && graph[u][v] && dist[u]! = INT_MAX
                        && dist[u]+graph[u][v] < dist[v])
                dist[v] = dist[u] + graph[u][v];
    }
        // print the constructed distance array
    printSolution(dist, V);
}
// driver program to test above function
int main()
{
    /* Let us create the example graph discussed above */
    int graph[V][V] = {{0, 5, 3, 0, 0, 0},
                {5, 0, 2, 5, 9, 6},
```

```
        {3, 2, 0, 0, 7, 0},
        {0, 5, 0, 0, 0, 8},
        {0, 4, 7, 0, 0, 9},
        {0, 6, 0, 8, 9, 0},
    };
    dijkstra(graph, 0);
    return 0;
}
```

2.6.   Priority Queues

Priority queue is an abstract data structure which can be implemented in multiple ways. Generally we implement priority queues using heaps. A priority queue is similar to stack and queue in which each element is associated with some priority. In priority queue the element with the maximum priority is accessed first and the element with the least priority is accessed last. Though the priority queues are implement using heaps, conceptually priority queues are different from heaps. A priority queue can be represented using unordered arrays and doubly linked lists.

2.6.1. *Operations on Priority Queues*

Push (): Inserts some element into priority queue.

Pop (): Removes an element with the least priority.

Peek (): Returns an element with the top priority.

Insert (item, priority): Inserts an element with the priority.

Get Highest Priority (): Returns the highest priority item.

Delete Highest Priority (): Removes the highest priority item.

Empty (): function returns whether the queue is empty.

Size (): function returns the size of the queue.

top (): Returns a reference to the top most element of the queue.

swap (): This function is used to swap the contents of one priority queue with another Priority queue of same type and size.

Value Type: Represents the type of object stored as an element in a priority queue. It acts as a synonym for the template parameter.

2.6.2. *Performance Comparison*

Data structure used for implementation	Insertion	Deletion	Search
Array	O (1)	O(n)	O(n)
Heaps	O (1)	O(logn)	O(logn)

Representation of Priority Queue Using Heaps

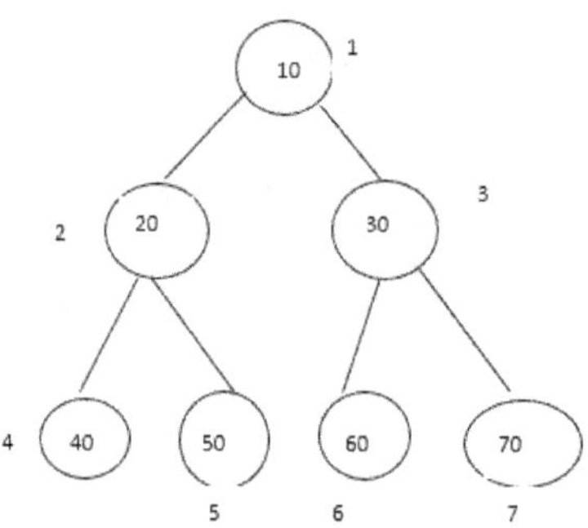

Figure 2.9: Heap Representation of Priority Queue

2.6.3. *Array Representation of Priority Queue*

In array representation, priority queue elements are used as an index for that element in the array. Means an element with priority 1 will be stored at index one, an element with the priority two will be stored at index two. Since no element will be there with priority 0, first slot in the array with index zero will be kept blank. In the below figure we can see the priority queue with array representation.

10	20	30	40	50	60	70
0	1	2	3	4	5	6	7

2.6.4. *Doubly Linked List Representation of Priority Queue*

To represent a doubly linked list we create a node with two link fields and two data fields. In which one data field is used to store the element and another one is used to store the priority.

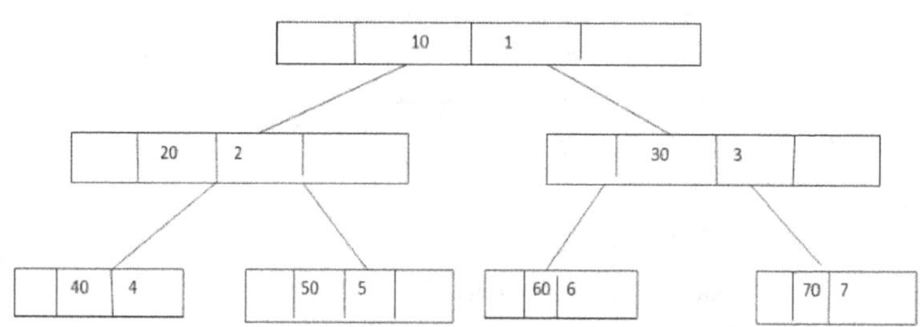

Figure 2.10: Doubly Linked List Representation of Priority Queue

2.6.5. *Algorithm for Implementation of Priority Queue Push Operation Using Doubly Linked List*

PUSH (HEAD, DATA, PRIORITY)

Step 1: Create new node with DATA and PRIORITY

Step 2: Check if HEAD has lower priority

If true follow Steps 3-4 and end

 else go to Step 5

Step 3: NEW -> NEXT = HEAD

Step 4: HEAD = NEW

Step 5: Set TEMP to head of the list

Step 6: While TEMP -> NEXT != NULL and TEMP -> NEXT -> PRIORITY > PRIORITY

Step 7: TEMP = TEMP -> NEXT

[END OF LOOP]

Step 8: NEW -> NEXT = TEMP -> NEXT

Step 9: TEMP -> NEXT = NEW

Step 10: End

2.6.6. *Algorithm for Implementation of Priority Queue Pop Operation Using Doubly Linked List*

POP (HEAD)

Step 1: Set the head of the list to the next node in the list. HEAD = HEAD -> NEXT

Step 2: Free the node at the head of the list

Step 3: End

2.6.7. *Algorithm for Implementation of Priority Peek Operation Using Doubly Linked List*

PEEK (HEAD):

Step 1: Return HEAD -> DATA

Step 2: End

Below is the Implementation of the Algorithm

```
// C# code to implement Priority Queue
// using Linked List
using System;
```

```java
class GFG
{
// Node
public class Node
{
    public int data;
      // Lower values indicate
    // higher priority
    public int priority;
      public Node next;
}
  public static Node node = new Node();
 // Function to Create A New Node
public static Node new Node (int d, int p)
{
    Node temp = new Node();
    temp.data = d;
    temp.priority = p;
    temp.next = null;
      return temp;
}
// Return the value at head
public static int peek(Node head)
{
    return (head).data;
}
// Removes the element with the
// highest priority form the list
public static Node pop(Node head)
{
    Node temp = head;
    (head) = (head). next;
    return head;
}
```

```java
// Function to push according to priority
public static Node push(Node head,
            int d, int p)
{
   Node start = (head);
    // Create new Node
   Node temp = newNode (d, p);
    // Special Case: The head of list
   // has lesser priority than new node.
   // So insert new node before head node
   // and change head node.
   if ((head). priority> p)
   {
       // Insert New Node before head
      temp.next = head;
      (head) = temp;
   }
   else
   {
       // Traverse the list and find a
      // position to insert new node
      while (start.Next! = null &&
         start.next.priority < p)
      {
         start = start.next;
      }
       // Either at the ends of the list
      // or at required position
      temp.next = start.next;
      start.next = temp;
   }
   return head;
}
 // Function to check is list is empty
```

```csharp
public static int isEmpty (Node head)
{
   return ((head) == null)? 1: 0;
}
 // Driver code
public static void Main (string[] args)
{
   // Create a Priority Queue
   // 7.4.5.6
   Node pq = newNode (4, 1);
   pq = push(pq, 5, 2);
   pq = push(pq, 6, 3);
   pq = push(pq, 7, 0);
    while (isEmpty(pq) == 0)
   {
      Console. Write ("{0:D} ", peek(pq));
       pq = pop(pq);
   }
}
}
```

Output:

    7 4 5 6

2.6.8. *Applications of Priority Queues*

1. **Bandwidth Management:** To allocate available bandwidth among the different category people we can use priority queues.
2. Used in various algorithms like prim's and kruskal to find the minimum cost spanning tree.

Important Short Answer Questions

1. Define what disjoint set is.
2. Write a short note on greedy method.
3. Write a short note on union and find algorithm.
4. What is 0/1 knapsack problem?
5. Define spanning tree.

6. Define minimum cost spanning tree.

7. What is single source shortest path problem?

8. What is priority queue?

9. What is the difference between a priority queue and a normal queue?

10. What operations are allowed on priority queues?

Important Essay Questions

1. Explain about 0/1 knapsack problem in details. Explain the greedy approach to solve the 0/1 knapsack problem using an example.

2. Explain about priority queues in details.

3. Explain in detail about single source shortest path problem using an example.

4. Explain in detail about job sequencing problem with deadline using an example.

5. Explain in detail about kruskal's approach to find the minimum cost spanning tree.

6. Explain in detail about the dijkstra approach for finding the single source shortest path problem.

Unit III

Dynamic and Back Tracking Approaches to Problem Solving

3. Key Objectives

In this unit we are going to study in detail about dynamic programming and back tracking techniques along with the different applications of those techniques.

3.1. Dynamic Programming

Dynamic programming technique is a problem-solving technique similar to greedy, divide and conquers techniques. The unique feature of dynamic programming is always produces optimal solution. Though it is slow it is efficient than greedy method because it guarantee an optimal solution every time. We know that greedy method is simple and easy to implement but there is no guarantee of getting optimal solution every time.

In dynamic programming approach a problem is always divided into sub problems, and again these sub problems are also divided into sub programs, this will be repeated until we get a sub problem which is solvable. The solutions of these sub problems are combined to find the solution to the original problem. Another interesting thing of dynamic programming is once a sub problem is solved the solution of that will be preserved with the expectation that these sub problems will be repeated in some other problems. If these are repeated again that time there is no need of solving it once again we can use the preserved solutions this concept is known as memorization. With this memorization concept only dynamic programming could solve the problems quickly.

3.1.1. Applications of Dynamic Programming

1. Travelling Sales Person Problem

A travelling sales person always starts from his/her home town and visits all the nearby villages to sell goods and finally in the evening try to come back to his town. Here the problem is about finding minimum cost path to finish his tour. The distances between the villages is fixed and given to us so that we can find a cycle with minimum cost. Here we should note that the cycle is not a Hamilton because for a given graph there is a possibility of having multiple Hamilton cycles, so we should try to find the Hamilton cycle with minimum cost also known as a minimum weighted Hamilton cycle.

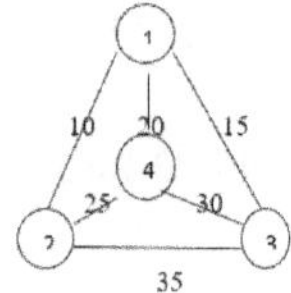

Figure 3.1: Graph P

For the above graph minimum weighted Hamilton cycle is 1-2-4-3-1.

Cost of the minimum weighted Hamilton cycle is = 80.

The above problem is a NP-hard problem because it can't be solved in polynomial time. There are several solutions to travelling sales person problem. The problem can be solved using following different approaches like.

1. Naïve Approach
2. Dynamic Programming
3. Triangle Inequality

Naïve Approach

Step 1: Consider city 1 as the starting and ending point for the tour.

Step 2: Generate all (n-1)! Permutations of cities.

Step 3: Calculate the cost of every permutation and keep track of the minimum cost permutation.

Step 4: Return the permutation with minimum cost.

Time Complexity of this solution is O (n!).

Dynamic Programming

To solve this kind of problems in dynamic programming approach we have an algorithm known as approximate algorithm. The approximate algorithm internally uses prim's algorithm to find the minimum cost spanning tree.

Approximate Algorithm

Step 1: Let vertex 1 be the starting and ending point for the salesman.

Step 2: Construct the MCST with 1 as the root using prim's algorithm.

Step 3: List all vertices in the preorder walk of the MCST and add 1 at the end.

Example: Consider the following graph. The graph represents that there are five villages including the home village / town of the sales person. Assume that village 1 is the home village of the sales man. Means village one is the starting and ending point for the sales man. In this problem the distances among the villages are also given based on that here we are requested to find the minimum cost route.

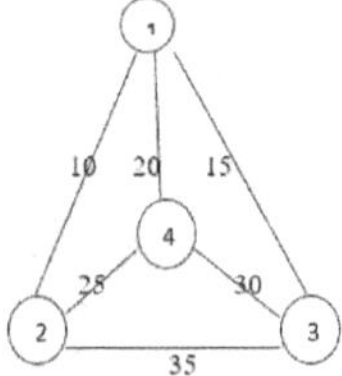

Figure 3.2: Graph R1

Step 1: We assume 1 as the sales person home village.

Step 2: Find the MCST using Prim's algorithm.

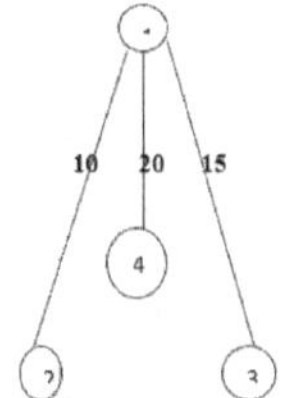

Figure 3.3: Graph R2

Step 3: Preorder traversal of the MCST is 1-2-4-3.

Step 4: Add 1 in the ending of the Preorder traversal of the MCST is 1-2-4-3.

Step 5: Minimum cost path to finish his tour is 1-2-4-3-1.

Exercise 1: There is a sales person named James his home town is 1. Every day he starts from village 1 and visits the nearby villages 2,3,4,5 and 6 to sell his goods. If he wishes to reduce his travelling expenditure suggest a route which will finish his tour in less time and cost. Try to find the solution to the following travelling sales person problem.

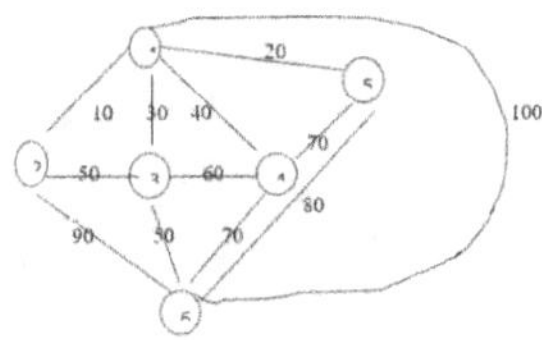

Figure 3.4: Graph S

Exercise 2: In the village A there is a family of Ramu. His family was very big, he used to live with his five sons, 8 daughters, parents and his wife Latha in rented house. For his livelihood we used to work in a departmental store and other family members used to prepare pillows. As the departmental store was closed on the Sunday's he used to room in the streets of B, C, D, E, F and

G to sell the pillows. As he is not so cleaver used to spend most of the earnings in the travelling itself. Try to suggest him an optimal path to finish his tour. The distances between the villages are fixed and give to us. Distances between A and C is 10 km, A and B is 20, C and D is 20, G and E is 23, B and F is 30, D and E are 10, E and F is 40. There is also a direct path from A to E, its distance is 25.

3.2.   Optimal Binary Search Trees

Optimal binary Search tree is binary search tree with the minimum search time. To construct the optimal binary search tree most commonly we prefer dynamic program approach because it guarantees an optimal solution every time.

Ex: 10, 20, 30

Possible binary trees with the above keys are 2nCn/n+1

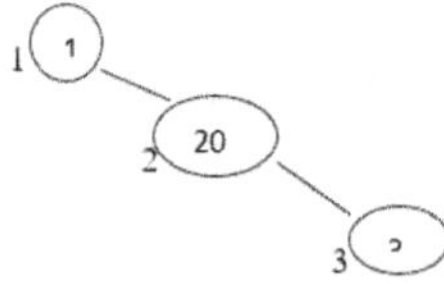

Figure 3.5: Graph 01

No of trials required to access element 10 is 1

No of trials required to access element 20 is 2

No of trials required to access element 30 is 3

Average access time of the above priority queue is 3

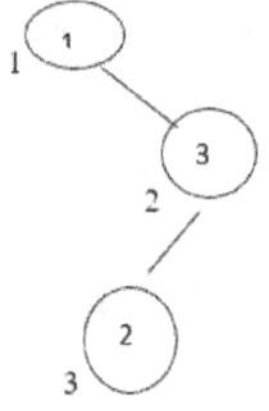

Figure 3.6: Graph 02

No of trials required to access element 10 is 1

No of trials required to access element 30 is 2

No of trials required to access element 20 is 3

Average access time of the above priority queue is 3

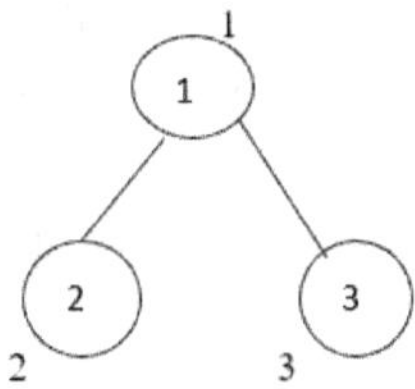

Figure 3.7: Graph 03

No of trials required to access element 1 is 1

No of trials required to access element 20 is 2

No of trials required to access element 30 is 2

Average access time of the above priority queue is 2.5

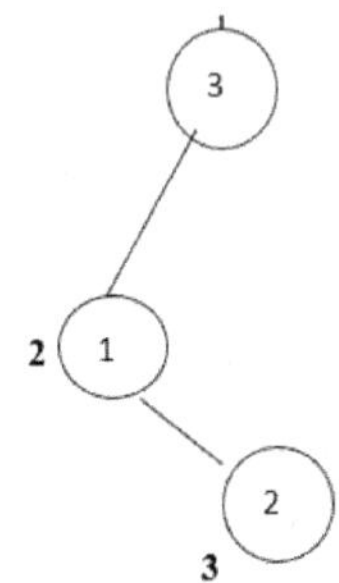

Figure 3.8: Graph 04

No of trials required to access element 30 is 1

No of trials required to access element 10 is 2

No of trials required to access element 20 is 3

Average access time of the above priority queue is 3

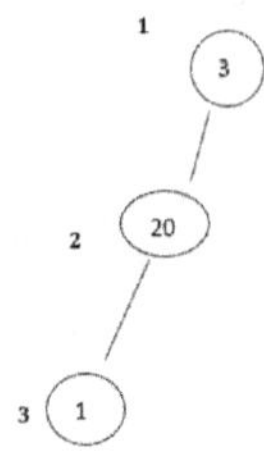

Figure 3.9: Graph 05

From the above five possible binary search trees of the given three elements we can say that the height balanced binary search tree is an optimal binary search tree but every height balanced binary search tree is not an optimal binary search tree. To cross verify this point let us proceed with the same elements once again, but this time I will add one more property to the elements that is its frequency.

Table 3.1: Binary Search Tree with Key Frequencies'

Element	Key	Frequency
1	10	5
2	20	4
3	30	2

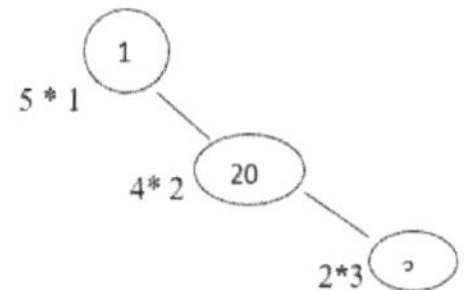

Figure 3.10: Graph 06

No of trials required to access element 10 is 1*5(no of trials * its frequency) = 5

No of trials required to access element 20 is 2= 4*2=8

No of trials required to access element 30 is 3=3*2=6

Average access time of the above priority queue is 19/11

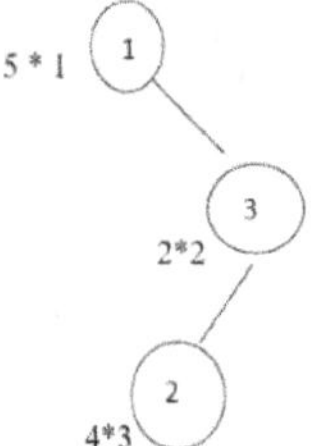

Figure 3.11: Graph 07

No of trials required to access element 10 is 1*5(no of trials * its frequency) = 5

No of trials required to access element 20 is 2= 4*3=12

No of trials required to access element 30 is 3=2*2=4

Average access time of the above priority queue is 21/11

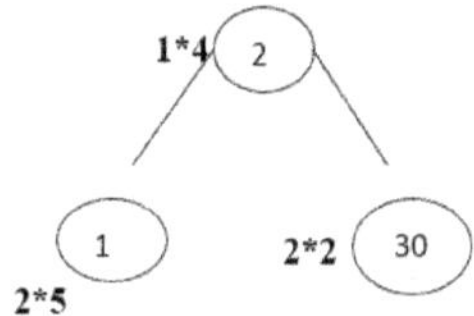

Figure 3.12: Graph 08

No of trials required to access element 10 is= 2*5(no of trials * its frequency) =10

No of trials required to access element 20 is= 1*4=4

No of trials required to access element 30 is=2*2=4

Average access time of the above priority queue is 18/11

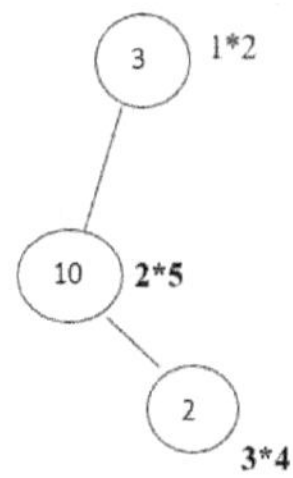

Figure 3.13: Graph 09

No of trials required to access element 10 is 2*5(no of trials * its frequency) =10

No of trials required to access element 20 is = 4*2=6

No of trials required to access element 30 is =3*4=12

Average access time of the above priority queue is 28/11

Note: T3 is an optimal binary search tree when frequencies are also considered.

To find the optimal binary search tree we generally use tabulation method in the dynamic programming.

Let us consider the following problem to find the optimal binary search tree using the tabulation method.

Table 3.2: BST with Key Frequencies

	1	2	3	4
Keys	10	20	30	40
Frequency	5	4	3	2

In tabulation method column index represents the 0/1 knapsack capacity. Row index represents the no of objects we should include into the knapsack.

Table 3.3: Tabulation Method to Find OBST

	0	1	2	3	4
0	0	5	13^1		
1		0	4	10^2	
2			0	3	8^4
3				0	2
4					0

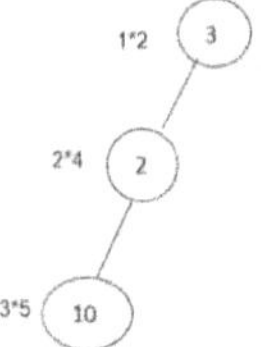

Figure 3.14: Graph O10

No of trials required to access element 10 is 3*5(no of trials * its frequency) =15

No of trials required to access element 20 is = 2*4=8

No of trials required to access element 30 is =1*2=2

Average access time of the above priority queue is = 25/11

3.3.   0/1 Knapsack Problem

0/1 Knapsack problem is all about arranging the given objects into the knapsack without exceeding the capacity of the bag in such a way to get the maximum profit. It is actually maximization problem so can be solved easily using dynamic programming. We know that 0/1 knapsack problem cab solved using greedy method also but an efficient way is using dynamic programming. In dynamic programming approach we have two methods (1) Tabulation method (2) Sets Method. Let us discuss about all these two methods to solve the 0/1 knapsack problem.

3.3.1.   Tabulation Method

Let us assume that there are four watermelons and we are requested to arrange these fruits in a 0/1 knapsack with the storage capacity of 8kg. The weight of the watermelons w1, w2, w3 and w4 is 1, 3, 4 and 5 respectively. The following table shows the list of objects and their associated profits.

Table 3.4: Knapsack with Profit & Weight

Profit	1	2	5	8
Weight	1	3	4	5

In tabulation method column index represents the 0/1 knapsack capacity. Row index represents the no of objects we should include into the knapsack.

Table 3.5: Tabulation Method to Find OBST

	0	1	2	3	4	5	6	7	8
0	0	0	0	0	0	0	0	0	0
1	0	1	1	1	1	1	1	1	1
2	0	1	1	2	3	3	3	3	3
3	0	1	1	2	5	6	6	7	7
4	0	1	1	2	5	6	6	9	10

Sets Method

$S^0 = \{(0, 0)\}$

$S^0 = \{(1, 1)\}$

$S^1 = S_0 U S^1_0 = \{(0, 0), (1,1)\}$

$S^1 = \{(2, 3), (3,4)\}$

$S^2 = s^1 U s^1_1 = \{(0,0), (1,1), (2,3), (3,4)\}$

$S^2_1 = \{(5, 4), (6,5), (7,7), (8,8)\}$

$S^3 = \{(0,0), (1,1), (2,3), (3,4), (5,4), (6,5), (7,7), (8,8)\}$

$S^3_1 = \{(8,5), (9,6), (10,8), (13,9), (14,10), (15,12), (16,13)\}$

$S^4 = \{(8, 5), (9, 6), (10, 8)\}$

3.4.   All Pairs Shortest Path Problem

All pairs shortest path problem is all about finding the shortest path between all vertices of a given graph. To solve this problem most commonly people will use dynamic programming. In dynamic programming approach we have a technique known as flody marshal which can be used for finding a solution for the all pairs shortest path problem. We know that using greedy method also we can solve this problem but greedy won't solve this problem efficiently. We have a greedy algorithm called Dijkstra can be used to solve this problem but for which we need to run the algorithm for N no of times, where N represents the no of vertices in the given graph G. Though the worst-case performance of the Dijkstra and flody both are same i.e., O (n3). We generally prefer flody warshall algorithm because in the best case and average case it takes less time compared with the dijkstra algorithm.

Ex:

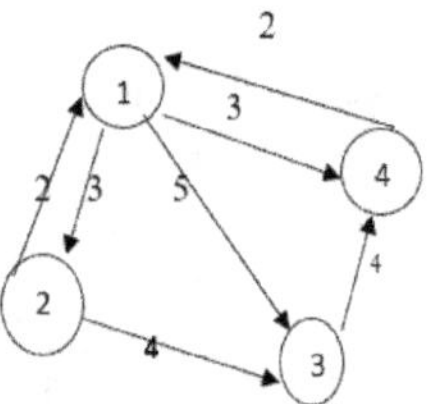

Figure 3.15: Graph A

Distance between the vertices of a graph can be represented using distance matrix.

$$A^0 = \begin{bmatrix} 0 & 3 & 5 & 3 \\ 2 & 0 & 4 & \infty \\ \infty & \infty & 0 & 4 \\ 2 & \infty & \infty & 0 \end{bmatrix}$$

Let us check is there any shortest path between the vertices of graph G via some vertex 1.

$$A^1 = \begin{bmatrix} 0 & 3 & 5 & 3 \\ 2 & 0 & 4 & 5 \\ \infty & \infty & 0 & 4 \\ 2 & 5 & 7 & 0 \end{bmatrix}$$

Let us check is there any shortest path between the vertices of graph G via some vertex 2.

$$A^2 = \begin{bmatrix} 0 & 3 & 5 & 3 \\ 2 & 0 & 4 & 5 \\ \infty & \infty & 0 & 4 \\ 2 & 5 & 7 & 0 \end{bmatrix}$$

Let us check is there any shortest path between the vertices of graph G via some vertex 3.

$$A^3 = \begin{bmatrix} 0 & 3 & 5 & 3 \\ 2 & 0 & 4 & 5 \\ \infty & \infty & 0 & 4 \\ 2 & 5 & 7 & 0 \end{bmatrix}$$

Let us check is there any shortest path between the vertices of graph G via some vertex 3.

$$A^4 = \begin{bmatrix} 0 & 3 & 5 & 3 \\ 2 & 0 & 4 & 5 \\ 6 & 9 & 0 & 4 \\ 2 & 5 & 7 & 0 \end{bmatrix}$$

Matrix A4 represents the shortest path among all the vertices of a given graph G using flody marshal algorithm.

3.5. Back Tracking

Back tracking is a problem-solving technique similar to dynamic programming. We know that the dynamic programming technique is generally used to find the optimal solution or the best solution for the problems which can be divided to sub problems. Whereas this back-tracking technique is used to find all the possible solutions for the given problem. There is no other technique available to find all the possible solutions of any given problem. To represent these solutions, we use solution tree or state space tree. Some problems like n-queens problem, sum of subsets problem, graph coloring problem are generally solved using backtracking technique.

3.5.1. N-Queens Problem

A problem of arranging n queens in the chess board of size n*n such that no two queens are under attack, means no two queens are placed in the same row, column, or diagonal. The state space tree for the N-queens problem will be very wider, complex and of size exponential so let us try to solve the 4-queens problem using backtracking. Before we proceed to solve 4 queens' problem, let us try to know what actually a 4 queen's problem is. The 4-queens problem is tiny n-queen problem, only difference is in n-queen problem there will be n no of queens, whereas in 4-queens problem there will be 4 queens. In 4-queens problem we will be trying to arrange those 4 queens in the chess board of size 4*4 such that no two queens are under attack. To solve this problem also we prefer backtracking approach. Let us draw a 4*4 table first. In the first row and first column we can place the first queen, after placing the first queen, we won't place the second queen in the same row. Move to second row, in the second row's first column we can't place the 2 queens, and in the second row's second column also we can't place the 2 queens because they both will be under attack. Next, we think of placing it in the second row's third column, and we can place the queen there with any problem. After placing the 2nd queen we think of placing the 3rd queen. But there is no place for 3rd queen because all the four cells are under attack by the remaining two queens. In this situation we think of changing the position of first and second queens, second queen can be placed in the 4th column of the 2nd row. After that we can place the third queen in the second column of the third row. When it is placed in the third row and second column then there will be place for the fourth queen. So again, we should think of changing the positions of 1,2 and 3 queens. If we remove 3rd queen from the third row second column there will be no safe place for the 3rd queen so we remove the second queen from the second row fourth column. Even then also there is no use because the entire cells we have tried for second queen. So we remove the first queen from the first row and fist column and place in the first row and second column. After that we can place the second queen in the second row's fourth column. And third queen in the third row and first column. Finally, this time we can place the fourth queen in the fourth row and third column. The solution we found for the 4 queens' problem can be seen the below table1. If we try once again by placing the first queen in the first row and third column, we can find one more solution. The second solution is as shown in the table 2. The second solution is exactly the mirror image of the first solution.

	Q2		
			Q2
Q3			
		Q4	

Table 1

		Q1	
Q2			
			Q3
	Q4		

Table 2

The solution of the 4 queens' problem can be represented using the state space tree or the solution tree. The solution tree of the above 4 queen's problem is as follows.

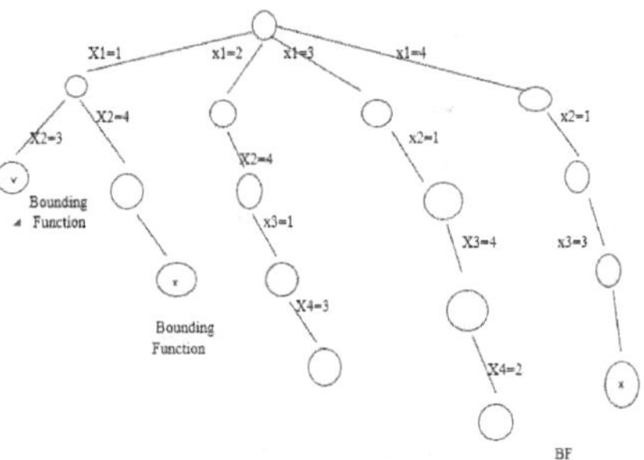

Figure 3.16: State Space Tree or Solution Tree

Solution 1:

Q1	Q2	Q3	Q4
2	4	1	3

Solution 2:

Q1	Q2	Q3	Q4
3	1	4	2

3.6.   Sum of Subsets

The sum of subsets problem is all about finding all the subsets such that their weights some is equal to the given weight. In this problem generally there will be n no of objects where each object is associated with some weight. And we are expected to find some subset, whose weight sum is equal to the given weight. To solve this problem there is an algorithm called exhaustive search. The exhaustive search algorithm first constructs the power set of the given set, and then it will try to pick the subset whose weight sum is equal to the given weight.

Example: Assume there are 4 objects whose weights are as follows, 10,20,30,40 and weight constraint is 50.

For this problem there will be only two solutions, they are {10, 40} and {20.30}. The exhaustive search algorithm is time consuming algorithm, so to solve this problem we use the back tracking. In the backtracking approach we will construct the state space tree to represent all the possible solutions. The state space tree or solution tree for the above problem using DFS algorithm is as follows.

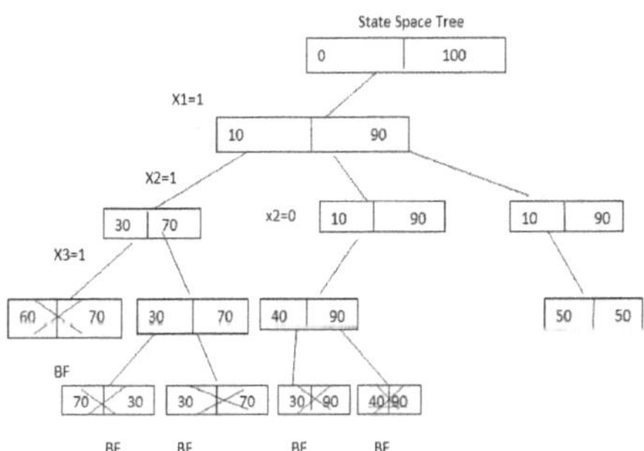

Fig. 3.17: State Space Tree or Solution Tree of Sum of Subsets Problem

Exercise 1: Assume there are 10 people with the age 53,45,81,12,47,49,42,25,23,47 and find the group of people whose total weight is 200. Try to find the all possible solution using sum of subsets technique in backing approach.

3.7.   Graph Coloring Problem

Graph coloring problem is all about coloring the different elements of a graph using the minimum no of colors such that no two adjacent elements have the same color. Each graph will have two elements known as the vertices and edges. On the basis of the elements of the graph, graph coloring problem is classified into two types. They are edge coloring problem and vertex coloring problem.

Edge coloring problem is all about coloring the different edges of the graph such that no two edges incident with the same vertex are colored in same.

Ex:

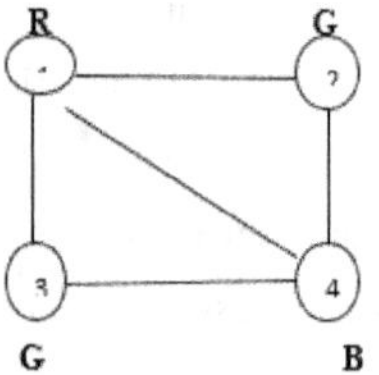

Figure 3.18: Graph G1

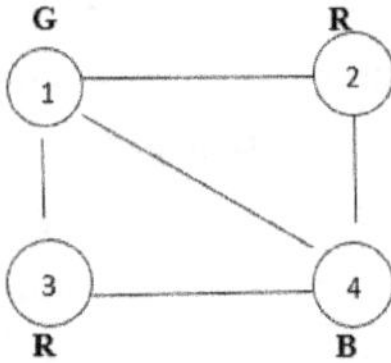

Figure 3.19: Graph G2

For graph coloring problem there will be more than one problem if we wish to find all those solutions then backtracking is the best solution.

State space tree for the above graph coloring problem is as follows.

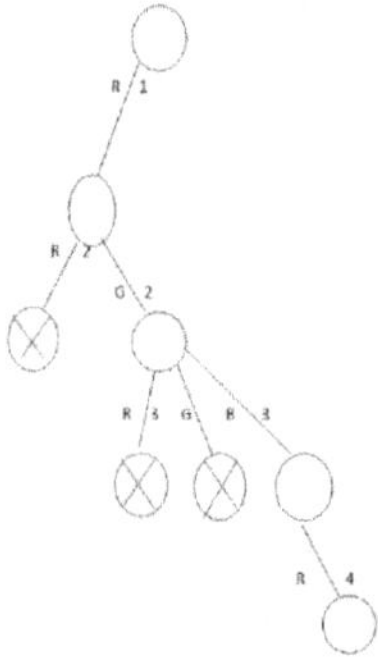

Figure 3.20: State Space Tree or Solution Tree

In the above state space tree, we can see one solution for the coloring the graph G. Like this if we try for the remaining options, we can get more results.

Exercise 1: Find the all possible solutions for the following graph coloring problem using backtracking technique.

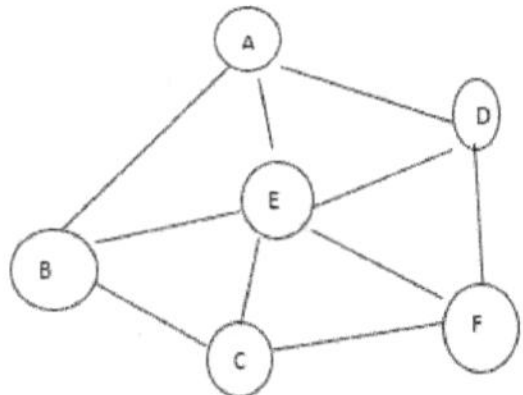

Figure 3.21: GC1

Exercise 2: Find the all possible solutions for the following graph coloring problem using backtracking technique.

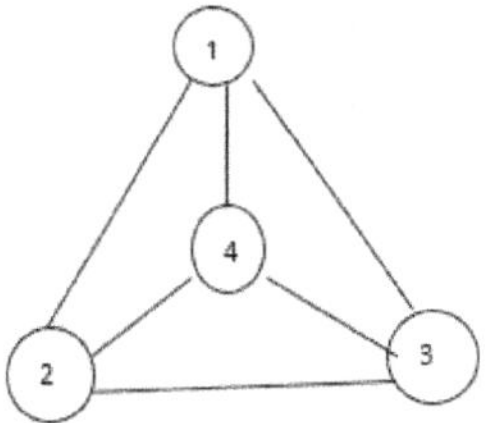

Figure 3.22: GC2

Important Short Answer Questions

1. What is Dynamic Programming?

2. What is Back Tracking?

3. What is travelling sales person problem?

4. What is optimal binary search tree?

5. What is 0/1 knapsack problem?

6. What is n queen's problem?

7. What is sum of subsets problem?

8. What is graph coloring problem?

9. Write a short note on tabulation method.

10. What is all pairs shortest path problem?

11. What is 4 queen problem?

1. Explain how dynamic programming approach is used to find a solution to the travelling sales person problem.

2. Explain how optimal binary search tree is found using dynamic programming approach using some example.

3. Explain the tabulation method to find the solution for the 0/1 knapsack problem.

4. Explain in detail about all pairs shortest path problem with an example.

5. Explain in detail how backtracking is used to solve the n queens' problem.

6. Explain how 4 queens' problem is solved using backtracking.

7. What is sum of subsets problem? Explain how sum of subsets problem is solved using backtracking with an example.

8. What is graph coloring? How a graph coloring problem can be solved using backtracking.

UNIT IV

LINEAR DATA STRUCTURES, SEARCHING AND SORTING TECHNIQUES

4. Key Objectives

In the first chapter we are going to learn about linear data structures like stack and queue and various operations can be performed on stack and queue. In the second chapter we are going to learn about hashing functions and different collision resolution techniques. In the third chapter we will learn about different sorting techniques.

Introduction

Data Structure is a specialized format for storing, organizing the data such that insertion and deletion operations can be done very efficiently. There are n no of data structures in the market but we need to pick the best one among them. If none of the available data structure is best suited for our application then we design a new data structure. Assume there is an application where we need to access the data in the order of their insertion then Queue is best suitable data structure. In the second application if we need to access data in the reverse order of their insertion then we need stack. Assume there is one more application in which we need to store the data along with no of times we have accessed that data item and the time when it was accessed for which there is no suitable data structure so in this case we need to design a fresh data structure with the help of the available data structures.

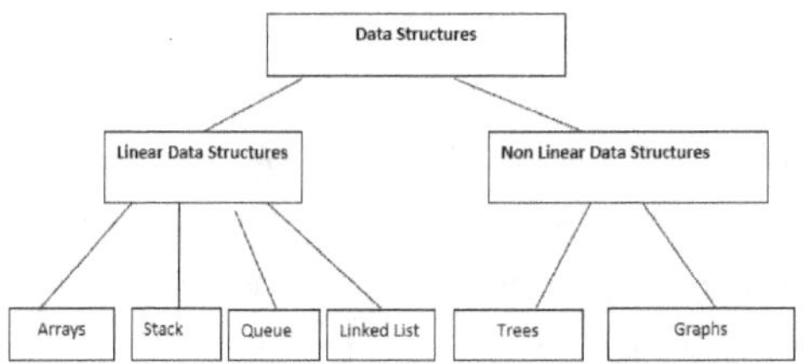

Figure 4.1: Data Structures Classification

Data structures are basically divided into two types. They are linear data structures and nonlinear data structures.

Linear data structures are those data structure which are used to store and organize the data in a linear sequence. In these data structures data is actually stored in the consecutive memory locations. Because of that only we can access data only in a sequential order. Linear data structures are very easy to implement and we can visit or traverse all the data items in a single run. In linear data structures all the data items are of the same level and there will be no hierarchical relationship among them.

Ex: Arrays, Stacks, and Queues.

4.1.   Array

Arrays are the best example for linear data structures, in which a set of data items will be stored in the consecutive memory locations, these data items are of the same type and share the same name. To access the individual elements of an array we use an index variable known as the array index. Array index generally begins with 0 and ends with n-1 where n represents the size of the array.

Ex:

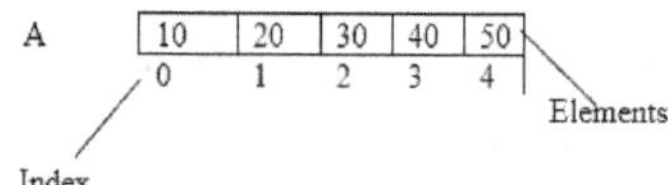

4.2.   Stack

Stack is a linear data structure in which elements are stored on one on the anther. The element which is inserted first into the stack will be in the bottom and the element which is inserted last will be on the of the stack because this reason the elements which are inserted last are accessed first and the elements which are inserted last are accessed first. So it is called as FIFO data structure. FIFO means First In First Out. Some people also call it as LILO data structure. LILO stands for last in last out. To point out the top element in the stack we use a pointer variable known as Top. Top will holds zero value when the stack is empty, when an element is inserted into the stack immediately the top pointer value will be incremented by one. Similarly, when an item is removed from the stack the top pointer value will be decremented by 1. Inserting the elements into the stack is known as push operation and removing the elements from the stack is known as pop operation. While inserting a new element into the stack we need to verity whether the stack capacity is exhausted or not. If the stack capacity is exhausted then certainly we can't insert a new element into the stack which is known as the stack overflow. Similarly, while removing some element from the stack also we need to check whether the stack is empty or not. If the stack is empty still we look to remove some element from the stack in that situation we can't remove which is known as stack underflow.

4.2.1. *Operations on Stack*

Most common operations performed on the stack are known as push, pop, peek and search.

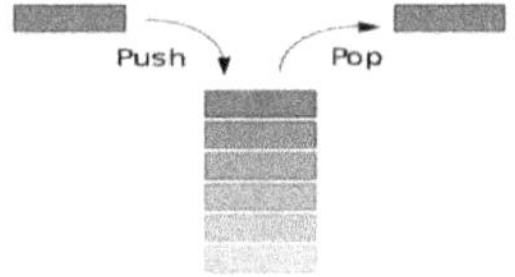

Figure 4.2: Stack

Push (): Push operation will simply insert some new element into stack if possible.

Pop (): Pop operation will simply remove top most element of the stack.

Peek (): Peek operation will give us the top most elements from the stack.

Search (): Search operation is used to check whether the search element is there or not.

Is empty (): Is-empty function is used to know whether the stack is empty or not. If the stack is empty it will return true otherwise it returns false value.

Is full (): Is full is used to know whether the stack is full or not. If the stack is full it returns true, otherwise it returns false.

Get-size (): Get size function is used to know the size of the stack. Size is nothing but the no of elements in that stack.

Ex: Assume there is a stack with 4 elements (a, b, c and d) and stack capacity is 8. Then we have performed two pop operations followed by two push operations to insert e and f. So now how many elements will be there and what are they.

Sol: Initially stack was with four elements as follows.

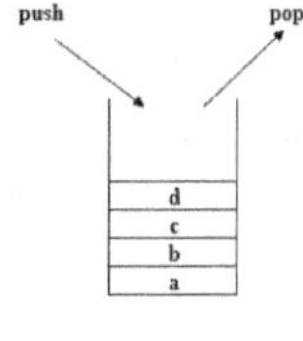

Top=3

Figure 4.3: Stack After Four Push Operations

After two pop operations performed on the above stack the top elements c and d were removed. The result of the two operations we can see in the following figure.

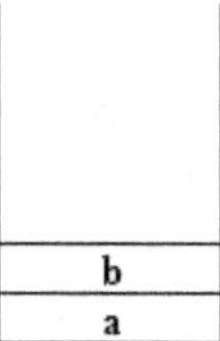

Top=1

Figure 4.4: Stack After Two Pop Operations

After two pop operations were performed, two push operations are performed to insert e and f.

Result of the two push operations we can see in the following figure.

Note: When the stack is empty top will be pointing to -1.

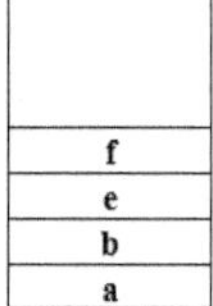

Top = 3

Figure 4.5: Stack After Push Operations

4.2.2. *Applications of Stack*

1. Stack can be used to reverse a given string.
2. For the implementation of undo operation in the text editors.
3. To know whether an arithmetic expression is balanced or not.
4. For converting the arithmetic expressions from prefix to postfix, postfix to prefix and infix to postfix or prefix and vice versa.
5. For the implementation Depth First Search graph traversal algorithm.
6. Used in all the applications where we want to access the data in the reverse of their insertion.
7. It is used in the implementation of recursions.
8. It is used in language processing for providing space to the local variables internally.
9. It also used to store the return address of the subroutine when the control is transferred from calling function to the called function.

4.2.3. *Program to Demonstrate Stack Operations*

```cpp
#include <iostream>
using namespace std;
int stack[100], n=100, top=-1;
void push(int val) {
  if(top>=n-1)
    cout<<"Stack Overflow"<<endl;
  else {
    top++;
    stack[top]=val;
  }
}
void pop() {
  if(top<=-1)
    cout<<"Stack Underflow"<<endl;
  else {
    cout<<"The popped element is "<< stack[top] <<endl;
    top--;
  }
}
void display() {
  if(top>=0) {
    cout<<"Stack elements are:";
    for (int i=top; i>=0; i--)
      cout<<stack[i]<<" ";
      cout<<endl;
  } else
    cout<<"Stack is empty";
}
int main() {
  int ch, val;
```

```cpp
cout<<"1) Push in stack"<<endl;
cout<<"2) Pop from stack"<<endl;
cout<<"3) Display stack"<<endl;
cout<<"4) Exit"<<endl;
do {
  cout<<"Enter choice: "<<endl;
  cin>>ch;
  switch(ch) {
    case 1: {
      cout<<"Enter value to be pushed:"<<endl;
      cin>>val;
      push(val);
      break;
    }
    case 2: {
      pop();
      break;
    }
    case 3: {
      display();
      break;
    }
    case 4: {
      cout<<"Exit"<<endl;
      break;
    }
    default: {
      cout<<"Invalid Choice"<<endl;
    }
  }
} while(ch! =4);
```

        return 0;

    }

Output:

1) Push in stack

2) Pop from stack

3) Display stack

4) Exit

Enter choice: 1

Enter value to be pushed: 2

Enter choice: 1

Enter value to be pushed: 6

Enter choice: 1

Enter value to be pushed: 8

Enter choice: 1

Enter value to be pushed: 7

Enter choice: 2

The popped element is 7

Enter choice: 3

Stack elements are:8 6 2

Enter choice: 5

Invalid Choice

Enter choice: 4

Exit

Complexity Analysis

Push: $O(1)$ Pop: $O(1)$ Size: $O(1)$

4.3. Queue

Queue is a linear data structure like stack which is also used to store some elements. The elements of the queue are related but nonhierarchical elements. Queue is a FIFO (First in First Out) or LILO (Last In Last Out) data structure means the elements which are inserted first are removed first or the elements inserted last are remove last. To follow FIFO order it uses to pointers known as the front and rear. The Front pointer always pointing to the first element in the queue and the pointer Rear will be pointing to the last element. When the queue is empty Front and Rear pointers both will maintains -1 value. Most common operations performed on the queue are enqueue and dequeue. Inserting some new element into the queue is known as enque and removing some element from the queue is known as dequeue operation. When some element is inserted into the queue the rear will be incremented by 1 and while removing some element from the queue first front will be incremented by 1 after that only element will be removed from the queue.

4.3.1. Queue Operations

Common operations performed on queues are:

Is empty (): Is used to know whether the queue is empty or not. If the queue is empty returns true else returns false.

clear (): Is used to clear the contents of the queue.

get First (): Is used to get the first element or the first element inserted into the queue.

get Last (): To get the last element in the queue.

enqueue (): Is used to insert some new element into the queue.

dequeue (): Is used to delete first element from the queue.

Ex: Perform the enqueue operation to insert the following elements a, b, c, d and perform two dequeue operations to remove two elements from the queue. Write the result of the above operations.

Sol: The following figure shows the initial state when the queue is created and empty. We know that when the queue is empty front and rear both will maintain the -1 value.

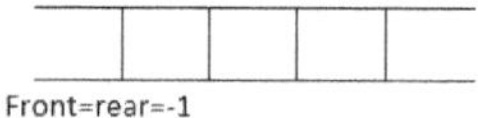

Figure 4.6: Empty Queue

When the first enqueue operation is performed, to insert that element into the queue first rear is incremented by one then the element is inserted with the help of the rear pointer and front will be maintaining the same value i.e., -1. Similarly, when the second enqueue operation is initiated the rear is incremented by one then the element is inserted into the queue and front will be same as -1. The result of the two enqueue operations we can see in the below figures.

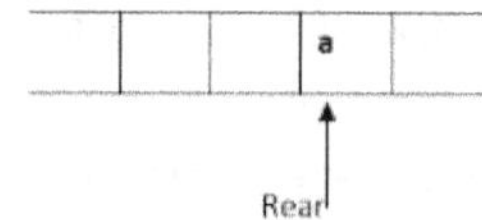

Figure 4.7: Queue with a Single Element

After four enqueue operations are performed, we have to perform two dequeue operations, the result of the two consecutive dequeue operations we can see in the figure below. When the first deque operation is initiated front will be incremented by one first and the element which is pointed by the front will be removed. When the deque operation is initiated once again on the queue front pointer value will be incremented by 1 and the value pointed by the front will be removed. The result of the two deque operations we can see in the figures below.

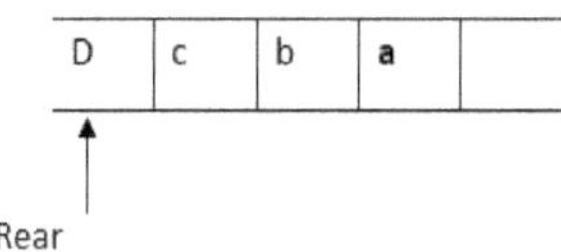

Figure 4.8: Queue with abcd Elements

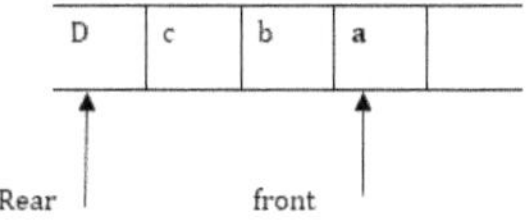

Figure 4.9: Queue with abcd Elements

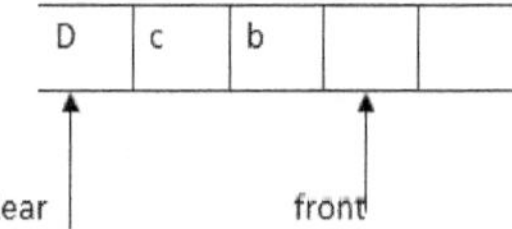

Figure 4.10: Queue with bcd Elements

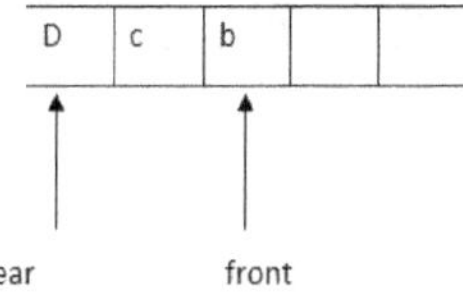

Figure 4.11: Queue with bcd

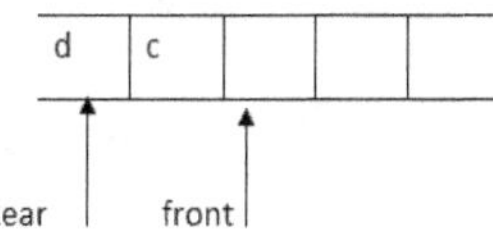

Figure 4.12: Queue with cd

4.3.2. *Algorithm for Enqueue Operation*

```
procedure enqueue(data)

   if queue is full
      return overflow
   endif

   rear ← rear + 1
   queue[rear] ← data
   return true

end procedure
```

Example for Enqueue Operation

```
int enqueue(int data)
   if(is full())
      return 0;

   rear = rear + 1;
   queue[rear] = data;

   return 1;
end procedure
```

4.3.3. *Algorithm for Dequeue Operation*

```
procedure dequeue

   if queue is empty
      return underflow
   end if

   data = queue[front]
   front ← front + 1
   return true
end procedure
```

Example for Dequeue Operation

```cpp
int dequeue() {
  if(is empty())
    return 0;

  int data = queue[front];
  front = front + 1;

  return data;
}
```

4.3.4. Program to Demonstrate Queue Operations

```cpp
/* Below program is written in C++ language */
#include<iostream>
using namespace std;
#define SIZE 10
class Queue
{
  int a[SIZE];
  int rear; //same as tail
  int front; //same as head
   public:
  Queue()
  {
    rear = front = -1;
  }
   //declaring enqueue, dequeue and display functions
  void enqueue (int x);
  int dequeue();
  void display();
};
// function enqueue - to add data to queue
void Queue:: enqueue (int x)
{
```

```cpp
    If(front == -1) {
        front++;
    }
    If(rear == SIZE-1)
    {
        cout << "Queue is full";
    }
    else
    {
        a[++rear] = x;
    }
}
// function dequeue - to remove data from queue
int Queue:: dequeue()
{
    return a[++front]; // following approach [B], explained above
}
// function to display the queue elements
void Queue:: display()
{
    int i;
    for(i = front; i <= rear; i++)
    {
        cout << a[i] << endl;
    }
}
// the main function
int main()
{
    Queue q;
    q. enqueue (10);
    q. enqueue (100);
    q. enqueue (1000);
    q. enqueue (1001);
```

q. enqueue (1002);

q. dequeue ();

q. enqueue (1003);

q. dequeue ();

q. dequeue ();

q. enqueue (1004);

q. display ();

return 0;

}

4.3.5. Types of Queues

We can classify the queues into four types, they are as follows.

1. Simple queues

2. Circular queues

3. Priority queues

4. Dequeues

4.3.5.1. Simple Queues

Simple queue is a normal queue which follows FIFO or LILO order.

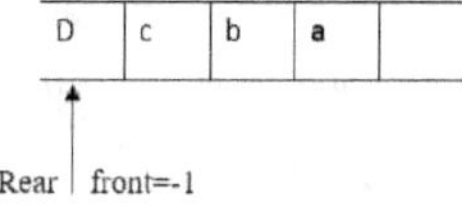

Figure 4.13: Queue with abcd Elements

4.3.5.2. Circular Queues

Circular queue is a special queue in which front end is connected to the rear end. In which insertion of some new element will be done in the end of the queue and deletion will be done from the front end. It is also known as ring buffer.

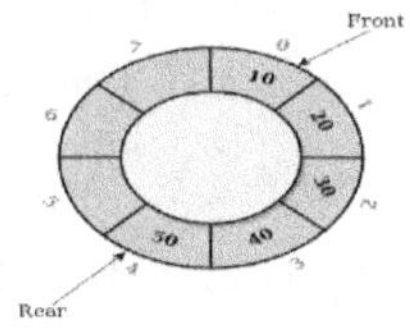

Figure 4.14: Circular Queue

4.3.5.3. *Priority Queues*

Priority queue is queue in which each element is associated with some priority. Elements are inserted in the order of their priority and removed on the basis of their priority. Generally, the elements with the minimum priority will be removed first from the priority queue. Conceptually, a priority queue is totally different from the normal queue.

4.3.5.4. *Dequeues*

Dequeue is nothing but doubly ended queue. In which insertion and deletion of elements can be done from the both ends.

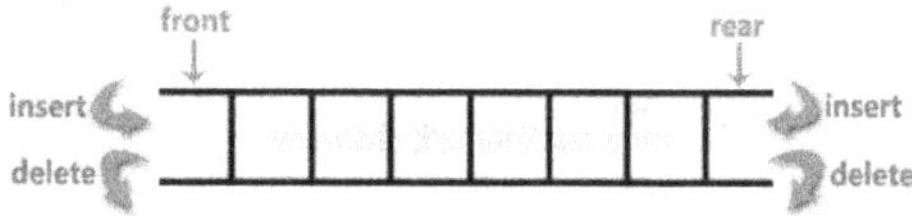

Figure 4.15: Dequeue

4.3.6. *Applications of Queues*

1. In the implementation of CPU scheduling algorithms.
2. In the implementation of disk scheduling algorithms.
3. For the asynchronous data transfer between two processes.
4. In the implementation of Breadth First Search traversal technique.
5. Used in all applications where we want to access the data in the order in which it is entered.

4.3.7. *Complexity Analysis*

Enqueue: **O (1)**

Dequeue: **O (1)**

Size: **O (1)**

4.4. Linked List

Linked list is a linear data structure similar to an array. A linked list contains a group of elements of similar type and these elements are not stored in the consecutive memory locations.

4.4.1. *Linked List Representation*

In liked list an element contains two fields i.e., data field and link field. In the data field, data is stored and in the link field the address of the next element is stored.

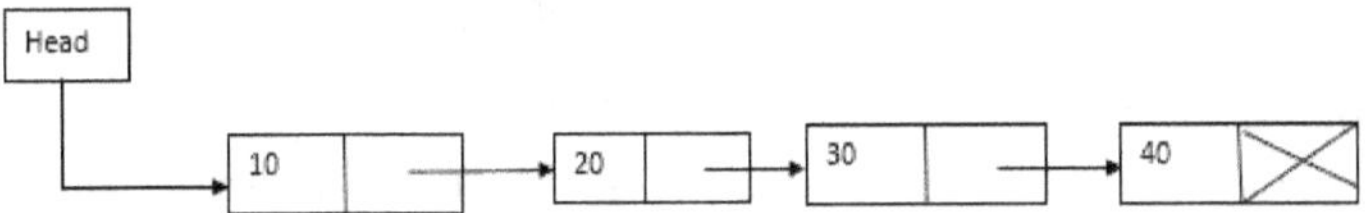

Figure 4.16: Single Linked List with Four Elements

Linked list uses a pointer known as the head, which will be always pointing to the first element of the linked list. In the first element's link field address of the second element is stored and in the link field of the second element, address of the third element is stored. And the last element link field maintains the null value.

4.4.2. *Insertion Operation*

To insert element 15 into the linked list, first we create a node with 2 fields and insert 15 into the data field, store the address of the node 20 into the link field of the node 15 and store the address of the node 15 into the link field of the node 10. By doing the above operation we can logically insert the node 15 in between the nodes 10 and 20.

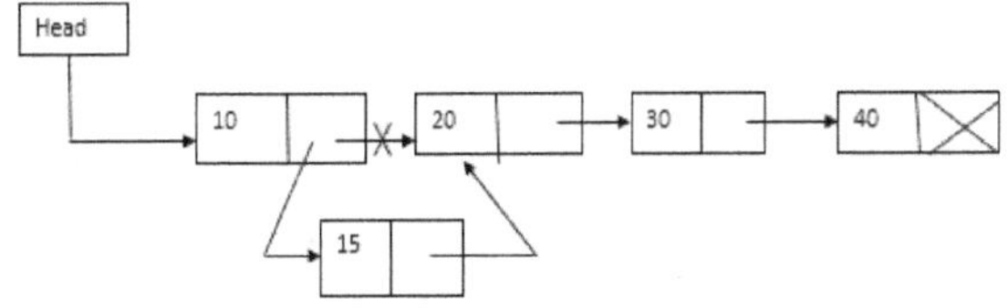

Figure 4.17: Inserting Element 15

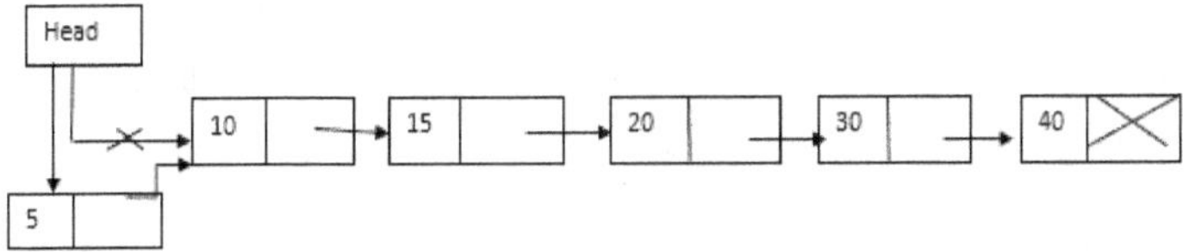

Figure 4.18: Inserting Element 5 in the Front

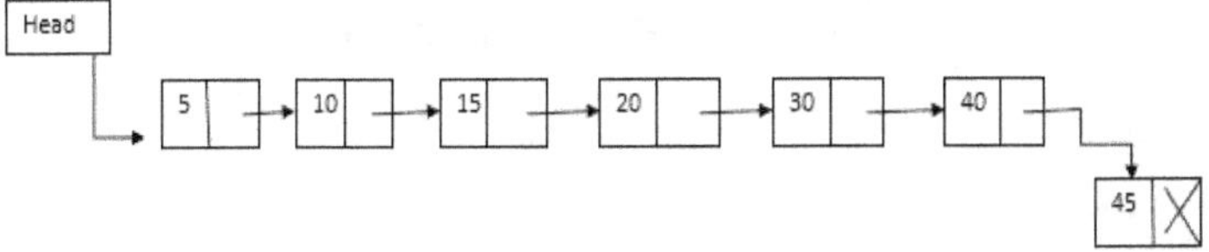

Figure 4.19: Inserting Element 45 in the End

4.4.3. Deletion of Some Element from the Linked List

To delete some element from the linked list what we need to do is, need to disconnect that element logically from the remaining elements. For example, assume we have to delete the element 15 from the below linked list. Then we simple place the address of the element 20 in the link field of the 10 which we de links the element 15 from the 10 and 20.

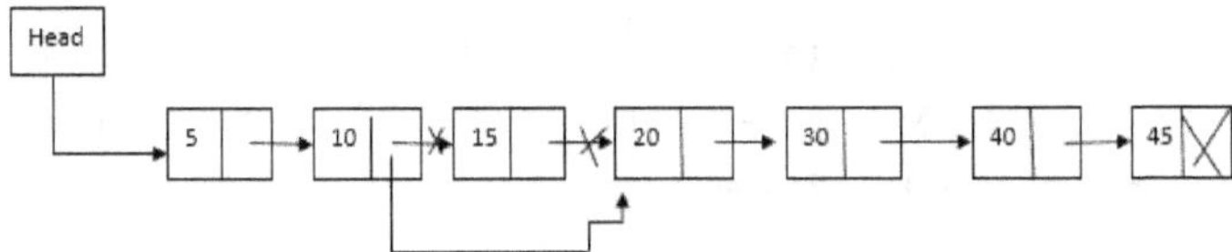

Figure 4.20: Deleting Element 15 from the Linked List

Resultant Linked list after removing element 15 is as follows:

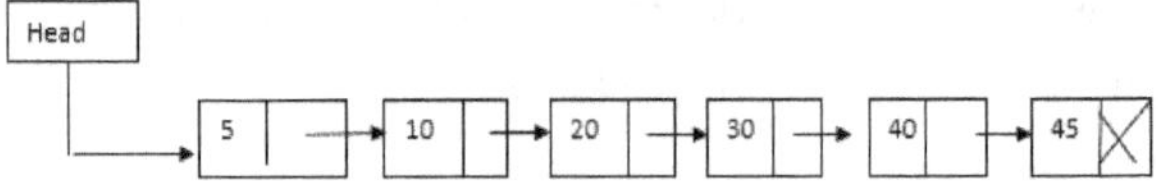

Figure 4.21: Linked List After Deleting Element 15

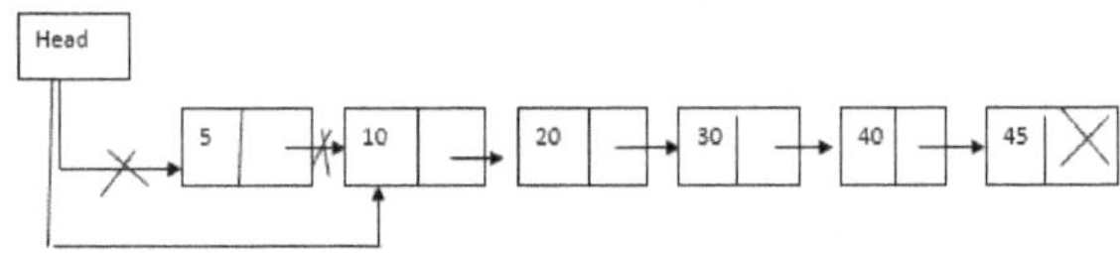

Figure 4.22: Deleting Element 5 from the Linked List

To delete 45 from the linked list just place the null value in the link field of the element 40 which will logically disconnect the node 45 from 40.

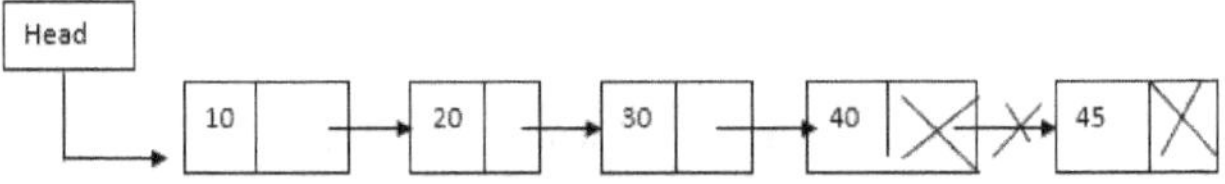

Figure 4.23: Deleting Element 45 from the Linked List

4.4.4. Circular Linked Lists

It is a linked list in which the last node is connected to the first node and first node is connected to the last node. Circular linked lists are two types, circular single linked list and circular double linked list.

1. **Circular Single Linked List:** It is a single linked list in which the link filed of the last node maintains the first node address so that we can move to the first node after visiting the last node.

Ex:

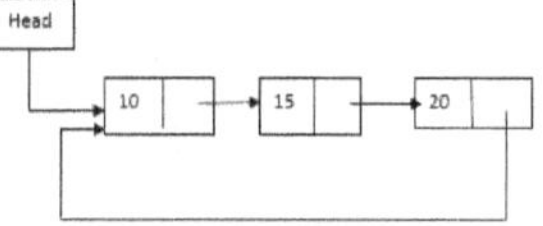

Figure 4.24: Circular Single Linked List

2. **Circular Doubly Linked List:** It is a doubly linked list in which the first node address is maintained by the last node and last node address is maintained by the first node. Because of this arrangement we can visit the last node immediately after visiting the first node and vice versa.

Ex:

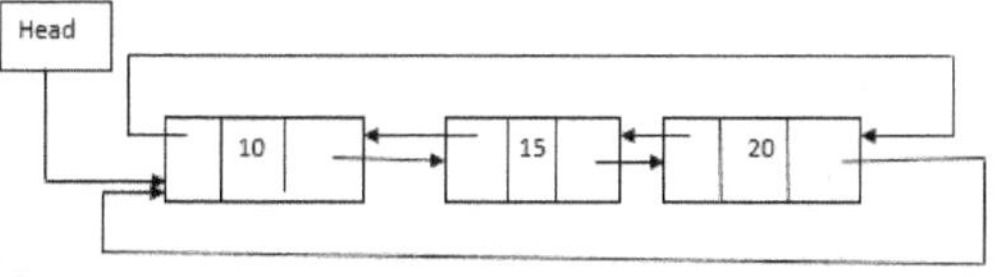

Figure 4.25: Circular Doubly Linked List

4.4.5. *Advantages of Linked Lists*

1. Size is not limited, it is infinite.
2. Insertion and deletion are done easily.

4.4.6. *Disadvantages of Linked Lists*

Random accessing of elements is not possible, it supports only sequential access.

4.4.7. *Applications of Linked Lists*

1. Used by operating system for dynamic memory allocation.
2. Used to represent very complex data structures like trees and graphs.
3. Used to perform arithmetic operations on polynomials.

4.5.   Hashing Technique

Hashing is an efficient technique for searching compared with the other searching techniques like linear search and binary search. The specialty of hashing is we can know whether that data item is available or not in a single attempt. To use hashing technique for searching we need to organize the data using hash table. Hash table is a two-field table, in which the field is index and second is data item.

Ex:

Index	Data Item
0	10
1	11
2	12
3	13

To insert, delete and search data from the hash table we apply some hash function on the hash table which is known as hashing. Most commonly used hash functions are division method, folding method and mid square method.

4.5.1. Division Method

In the division method to map a data item into the hash table, a mod function is applied on the data item.

Index = data item % hash table size

Ex: 15, 1, 25, 2, 35, 3, 4, 45

Assume the hash table size is 10 means there will be ten slots to accommodate ten data items.

Index	Data item
0	
1	1
2	2
3	3
4	4
5	15(25, 35,45 are also mapped to here which will cause the collision)
6	25
7	35
8	45
9	

In the above example data items 15, 25, 35 and 45 are mapped onto the same slot, which causes a collision, when there is a collision in the division method the data items are mapped on to the next empty slot. If there are some data items which are mapped on to the slots 6,7 and 8 are to be stored in the next empty slot. If there is no empty slot in the hash table the data item can't be accommodated successfully.

4.5.2. Mid Square Method

In the mid square method, the data item to be mapped into the hash table is squared first then the mid value is chosen as an index into the hash table.

Ex: 15, 1, 25, 2, 35, 3, 4, 45

Assume the hash table size is 10 means there will be ten slots to accommodate ten data items.

To accommodate the data item 15 into the hash table using mid square method first we square the data item 15, which is 225 so 2 will be chosen as an index for the data item. Similarly, 1 is mapped onto the slot with index 1. Data item 25 is mapped onto slot with index 2, but that slot is already occupied by data item 15 means there is a collision. To accommodate the data item 25 we use the next empty slot in the hash table, which is slot 4 with index 3. The data item 2 is mapped onto slot with index 4 because its square is 4. Next data item is 35, its square is 1225 but there is no slot with index 22. So again we square the data item 22, which is 484 means the data item 35 is to be mapped onto slot with index 8. The next data to be accommodated is 3, its square is 9 means it is to be accommodate at the slot with index 9. After 35, next data item is 4, its square is 16 but there is no slot with the index 16. So we will square the data index 16, its square is 256 means data item 4 is to be stored at the index 5. After 4 the last data item left is 45, its square is 2025 means it is mapped onto the slot with index 02 but which is already occupied by 15. So, we use the next empty slot i.e. is with the index 6.

Index	Data item
0	
1	1
2	15
3	25
4	2
5	4
6	45
7	
8	35
9	3

4.5.3. Folding Method

In the folding method to store some data item in the hash table, data item is divided into individual digits and these digits are added to get the index for that number.

Ex: 15, 1, 25, 2, 35, 3, 4, 45.

Assume the hash table size is 10 means there will be ten slots to accommodate ten data items.

First data item to be accommodated is 15 and its individual digits are 1 and 5. Sum of these digits is 6 means it is to be stored on to the slot with index 6. Next data item to be stored in the hash table is 1 means it is simply stored in the slot with index 1. The next data item to be stored is 25 and its individual digits are 2 and 5. Their sum is 7 means it is to be stored at the slot with index 7. Similarly the remaining data items 2, 35, 3, 4 and 45are mapped onto the slots with the index 2,8,3,4 and 9 respectively.

Index	Data item
0	
1	1
2	2
3	3
4	4
5	
6	15
7	25
8	35
9	45

4.5.4. *Collision Resolution Techniques*

Collision is a situation in which two or more than two data items are mapped onto the same slot in the hash table. In that situation the data item which is caused the collision can't be accommodated because it is already occupied by some other data item. To resolve this problem we have several collision resolution techniques known as linear probing or open addressing, quadratic probing, rehashing, double hashing and chaining.

1. **Linear Probing:** In this technique to resolve the collision the data item is simply mapped onto the next empty slot. Means addressing is open there are no restrictions on the mapping so it is also known as open addressing or open probing.

    Index = data item % hash table size

    New index = (index+1) % hash table size

2. **Quadratic Probing:** In quadratic probing if there is a collision data item will be mapped onto the perfect square of the previous index.

    New index = (index)^2

3. **Rehashing:** In this method whenever there is a collision to resolve the collision hashing will be performed once again on the incremented index.

    New Index = reshash (index+1) = (index+1) % hash table size

4. **Chaining Method:** In the chaining method there will be no collision situation occur because in which each slot maintains a single linked list. The data items which are mapped on to the slot with the same index are stored in the single linked list. For example, the data items which are mapped onto the slot with the index 0 are stored in the single linked list associated with the slot zero. The n represents the size of the hash table.

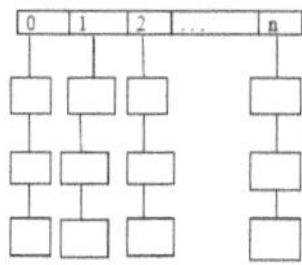

Figure 4.26: Hash Table Organization Using Chaining Method

5. **Double Hashing:** In double hashing to resolve the collision situation we use two hash functions.

New index = (hash1 (data) + I * hash2 (data)) % hash table size

hash1 (data item) = data item % hash table size

hash2 (data item) = PRIME - DATA ITEM % PRIME

4.6.   Sorting Techniques

Sorting is the process of arranging the elements either in ascending order or descending order. For sorting we have several techniques like merge sort, quick sort, insertion sort, selection sort, bubble sort, heap sort, radix sort and many more. Let us discuss in detail about all these sorting techniques one by one.

4.6.1. *Bubble Sort*

Bubble sort is one of the simple, easy to understand and implement sorting technique. Though it is simple, easy to understand and implement sorting technique we won't prefer it, because it is not an efficient sorting technique compared with quick sort and merge sort. In the best case it requires O (n) computation steps, in the average and worst cases it requires O (n²) computation steps.

Logic: In bubble sort every time we compare two adjacent elements, if they are in the expected order, we leave them as they are otherwise, we swap them. If there are n elements to be sorted then we require n-1 iterations. For each and every round we perform n-i comparisons where i, represents iteration number. The specialty of bubble sort is in this the smallest element will bubble up and largest element will sink.

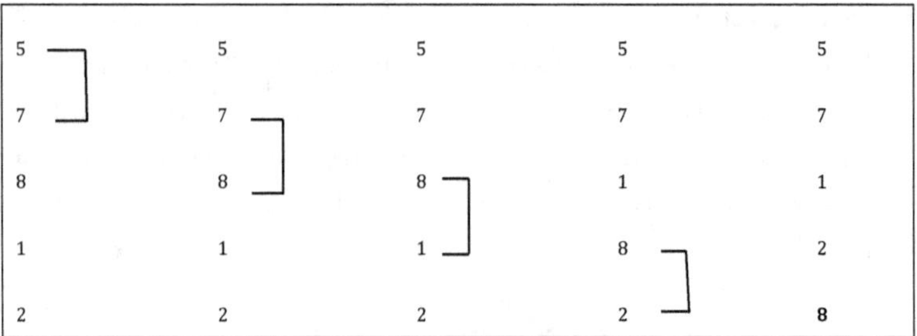

Figure 4.27: First Iteration

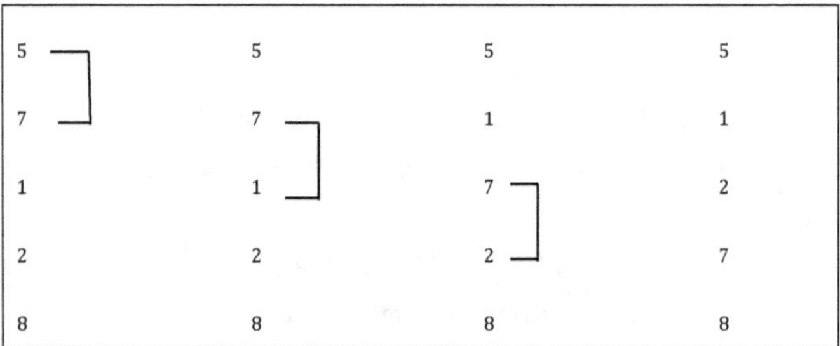

Figure 4.28: Second Iteration

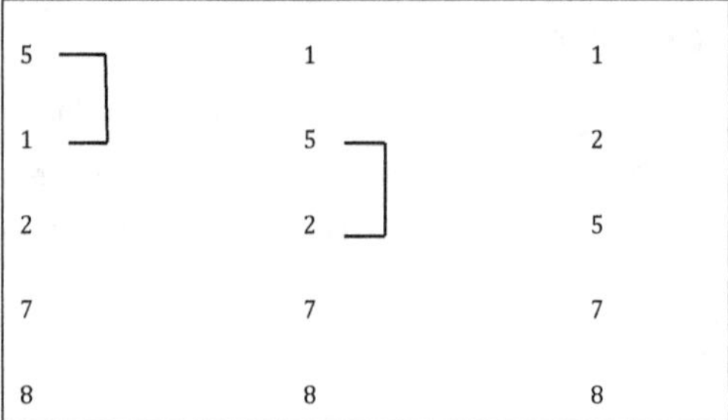

Figure 4.29: Third Iteration

Pseudo Code:

```
Bubble sort(int a[], int n)
 {
    for(i=0;i<n;i++)
      for (j=0;j<n-i-1;j++)
        {
          If(a[j]>a[j+1])
            Swap(a[j], a[j+1])
        }}
```

4.6.2. *Selection Sort*

Selection sort is a simple iterative and in place sorting technique. Selection sort logic is very interesting in this technique every time we pick a smallest element and try to place it in the appropriate place. If there are n elements to be sorted it takes n-1 iterations, in each iteration it takes n-I comparisons where I represents number of the iteration. Though selection sort is simple and interesting people won't prefer this because it takes $O(n^2)$ computational steps in the average and worst cases.

Ex: 10 1 25 2 35 3 4 45

- **First:** 1 10 25 2 35 3 4 45
- **Second:** 1 2 25 10 35 3 4 45
- **Third:** 1 2 3 10 35 25 4 45
- **Fourth:** 1 2 3 4 35 25 10 45
- **Fifth:** 1 2 3 4 10 25 35 45
- **Sixth:** 1 2 3 4 10 25 35 45
- **Seventh:** 1 2 3 4 10 25 35 45

In the given example in the first iteration we pick the first smallest element 1, which we will swap with the first element in the row. In the second iteration we pick the second smallest element 2 which we swap with the second element in the row. Similarly, in the third, fourth and fifth, sixth and seventh iterations we pick the elements 3, 4, 10, 25 and 35 and place in the respective positions.

4.6.2.1. *Selection Sort Algorithm*

Step 1: Initialize the min variable with zero.

Step 2: Pick the smallest element and place it in the appropriate location.

Step 3: Increment min by 1.

Step 4: Repeat from step2 until all the elements are sorted.

4.6.2.2. *Pseudo Code for Selection Sort*

```
Selection_sort (int a[], int n)
{
 Int min=0;
 For(i=0;i<n-1j;i++)
  {
```

```
For(j=i; j<n-i-1; j++)
        {
            If(a[j]<a[min])
                min=j;
        }
        Swap(a[i], a[min])
        min =min+1;
    } }
```

4.6.3. Radix Sort

Radix sort is one of the simple and efficient sorting techniques for large integers. It internally uses count sort technique and count sort is an efficient sorting technique only suitable for small integers. Radix sort is even efficient sorting technique than the merge sort, quick sort and heap sort techniques. Radix sort technique can be applied on decimals, binary numbers, octal, hexa decimal and strings also. It is a digit by digit sorting technique in which the sorting process will begin from the right most digit and ends with the left most digit. If there are n bit numbers to be sorted, it takes n iterations. Worst case performance of the radix sort is O(w*n).

Example: 1000 200 15000 50000 15

FIRST ITERATION	SECOND ITERATION	THIRD ITERATION	FOURTH ITERATION	FIFTH ITERATION
01000	01000	01000	50000	00015
00200	00200	15000	00015	00200
15000	15000	50000	00200	01000
50000	50000	00015	01000	15000
00015	00015	00200	15000	50000

4.6.3.1. Radix Sort Algorithm

Step 1: Do the following for each digit i where i varies from the least significant digit to the most significant digit.

Step 2: Sort the input array on the basis of i.

4.6.4. Insertion Sort

Insertion sort technique is one of the simple in place sorting technique. It is also called as internal sorting technique because it won't require additional memory for sorting the elements. To sort given n elements, it takes n-1 iterations. In this sorting technique every time pick some element and place it in the appropriate location. The logic of the insertion sort is similar to the playing cards game, in which also every time pick some new card and try to place it the appropriate place. Generally, people won't prefer insertion sort because of its performance. It's average and worst-case performance is O (n²).

Ex: 15 1 25 2 35 3 45 4

Sol: 15
1 15
1 15 25
1 2 15 25
1 2 15 25 35
1 2 3 15 25 35
1 2 3 15 25 35 45
1 2 3 4 15 25 35 45

Pseudo Code for insertion sort

```
Insertion_sort(int a[]; i<n;i++)
    {
        For(int i=1;i<n;i++)
        {
           Key=a[i];
           j=i-1;
           while(j>=0 &&a[j]>key)
              {
                  a[j+1] =a[j];
                  j=j-1;
              }
                  a[j+1] =a[j];
                  j=j-1;
        }
    a[j+1] =key;
    }
```

Important Short Answer Questions

1. What is stack?
2. What is stack overflow?
3. What is stack underflow?
4. Explain push and pop operations.

5. What is queue?

6. What is circular queue?

7. What is enqueue and dequeue?

8. What is array?

9. What is linked list?

10. How linked lists are represented.

11. What is hashing?

12. Explain hash table.

13. What is collision?

14. What is open addressing?

15. What is double hashing?

16. How collisions are resolved.

17. What is rehashing?

18. What is linear search?

19. What is binary search?

20. What is separate chaining?

21. How linked lists are represented.

Essay Questions

1. Explain in detail about stack and write a C++ program to implement stack operations.

2. Explain in detail about queue and write a C++ program to implement queue operations.

3. Explain in detail about linked list and write a C++ program to create a linked list.

4. What is hashing? Explain in detail about hash table.

5. What is collision? Explain different collision resolution techniques.

6. Explain in detail about bubble sort. Write a C++ program to sort a list of elements using bubble sort.

7. Explain in detail about selection sort. Write a C++ program to sort a list of elements using selection sort.

8. Explain in detail about insertion sort. Write a C++ program to sort a list of elements using insertion sort.

9. Explain in detail about radix sort. Write a C++ program to sort a list of elements using radix sort.

10. Explain in detail about heap sort. Write a C++ program to sort a list of elements using heap sort.

NONLINEAR DATA STRUCTURES

5. Key Objectives

In the present unit we are going to learn about nonlinear data structures like trees and graphs in detail. We also discuss about different tree and graph traversal techniques. In the end of this unit we will try to learn about different string-matching algorithms.

5.1. Nonlinear Data Structures

Nonlinear data structures are used to represent hierarchical data. For example, a family data, a department data and etc can be considered as hierarchical data. Nonlinear data structures are trees and graphs.

5.1.1. Trees

A tree is a nonlinear data structure, which may have zero nodes or it may have single designated node called root and zero or more sub trees. Trees are several types, like binary trees, binary search trees, AVL trees, Red and Black trees, B trees, B+ trees, and Splay Trees.

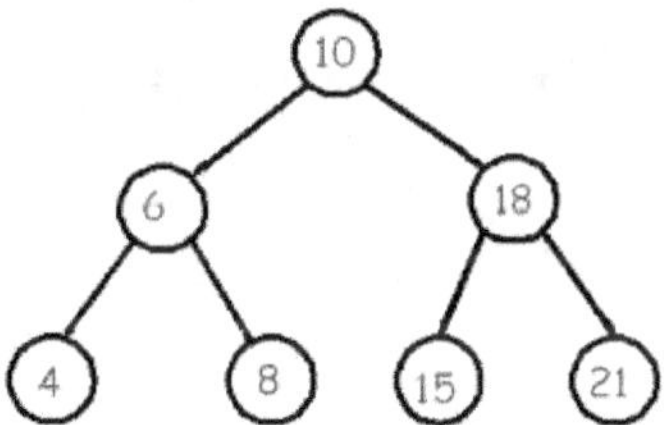

Figure 5.1: Binary Tree

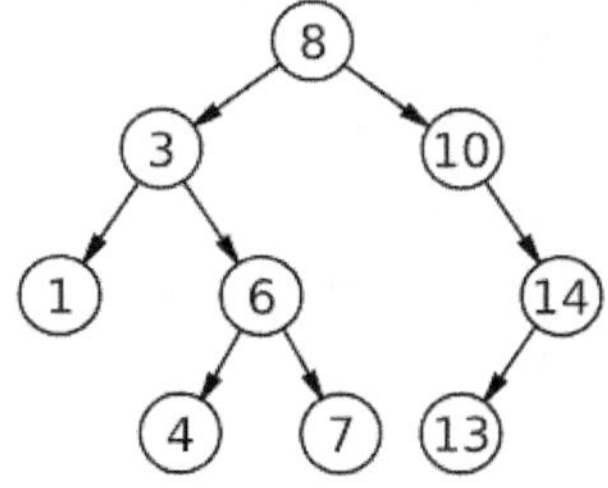

Figure 5.2: Binary Search Tree

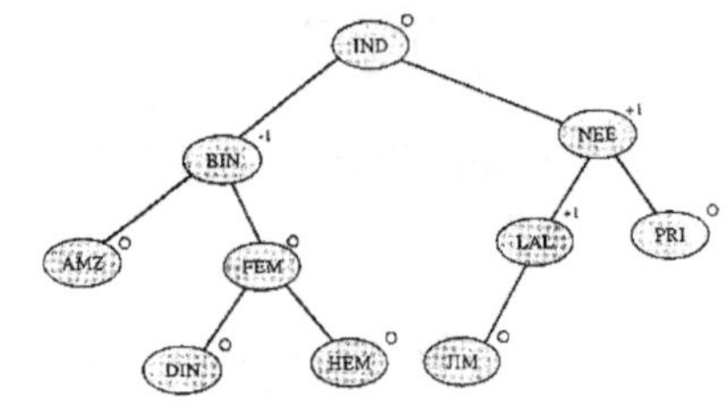

Figure 5.3: AVL Tree

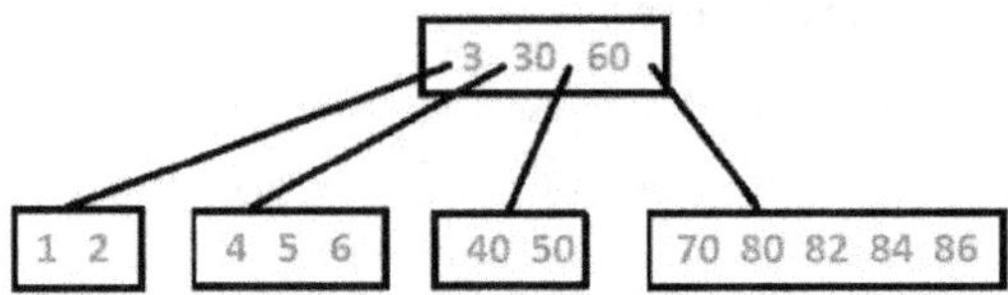

Figure 5.4: B Tree

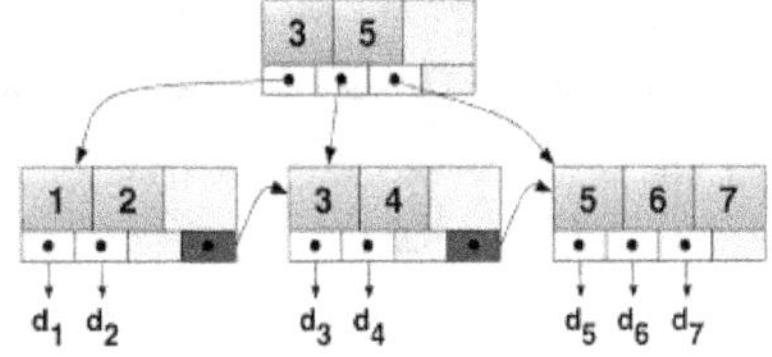

Figure 5.5: B+ Tree

5.1.2. Binary Trees

A binary tree is a tree in which each and every node will have at most two children. In which there will be a designated node called root and remaining nodes are divided into left sub tree and right sub tree.

1. In a binary tree if there are n nodes, then it may have exactly n-1 edges.
2. If a binary tree height is h then there will be at least h nodes and at most 2^h-1 node.
3. A binary tree with n elements will have at least n and at most $\log_2 (n+1)$ height.

Binary trees are also several types, they are:

1. Full binary tree
2. Perfect binary tree
3. Complete binary

4. Height balanced binary trees.

5. Degenerate binary tree or skewed trees and many more.

Full Binary Tree: A full binary tree is a binary tree in which each and every node will have at least two children.

Ex:

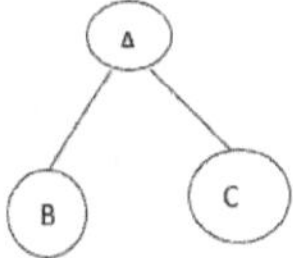

Figure 5.6: Full Binary Tree with 3 Nodes

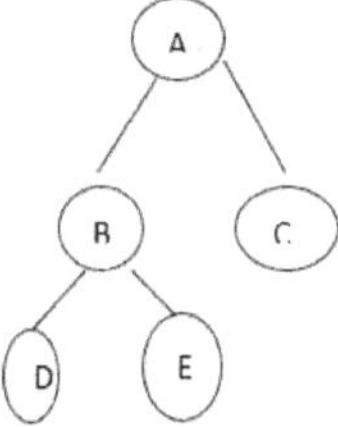

Figure 5.7: Full Binary Tree with 5 Nodes

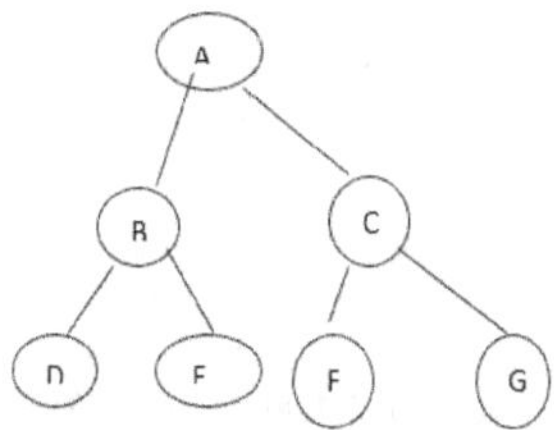

Figure 5.8: Full Binary Tree with 7 Nodes

Perfect Binary Tree: A perfect binary tree is a binary tree in which each and every node will have exactly two children and all leaves will occur at the same level. A perfect binary tree is a full binary tree in which all the leaves will occur at the same level. In the above figures A and B are not perfect binary trees and fig c is a perfect binary tree.

Complete Binary Tree: A complete binary tree is a binary tree in which each every node will have exactly two children except the last level nodes.

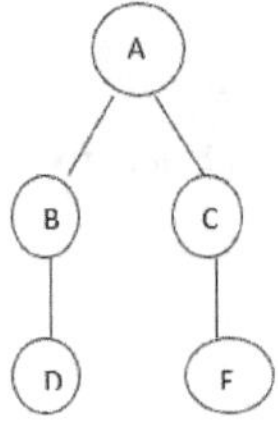

Figure 5.9: Complete Binary Tree with 5 Nodes

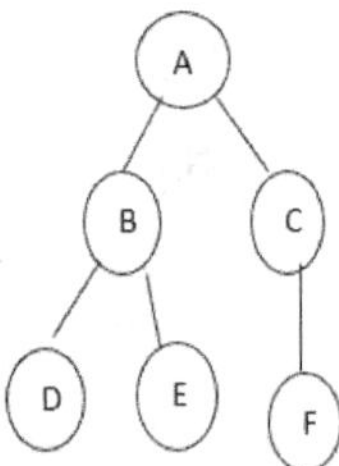

Figure 5.10: Complete Binary Tree with 6 Nodes

Height Balanced Binary Tree: A height balanced binary tree is a binary tree in which the height difference between the left sub tree and right sub tree is at most 1.

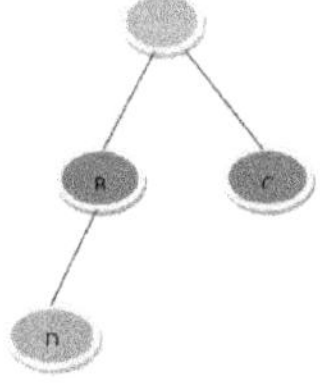

Figure 5.11: Left Heavy Height Balanced Binary Tree

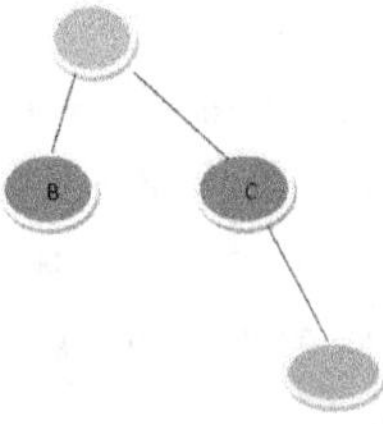

Figure 5.12: Right Heavy Height Balanced Binary Tree

Degenerate Tree: A degenerate tree is a binary tree in which each node will have exactly one child. A degenerate binary tree may be left skewed or right skewed.

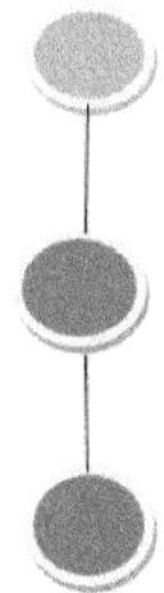

Figure 5.13: Degenerate Tree

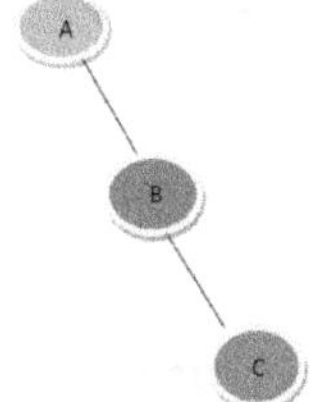

Figure 5.14: Right Skewed Binary Tree

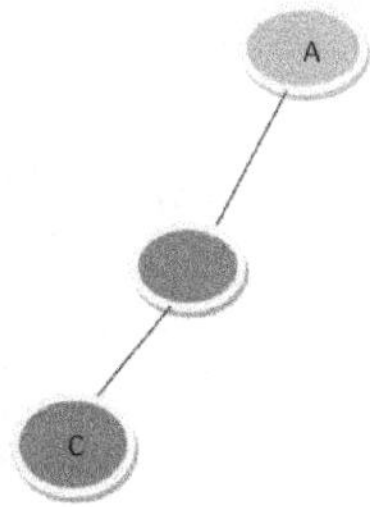

Figure 5.15: Left Skewed Binary Tree

5.1.3. Binary Tree Traversal Techniques

Tree traversal is nothing but visiting each and every node or vertices of a graph exactly once. Similarly, visiting the vertices of a binary tree is known as binary tree traversal. To traversal the binary trees we have four tree traversal techniques. They are as follows:

1. In order traversal technique
2. Pre order traversal technique
3. Post order traversal technique
4. Level order traversal technique

All the above four traversal techniques are recursive techniques.

In Order Traversal Technique: In the in-order tree traversal technique we will visit all the nodes in the following order:

1. Visit the left sub tree in order
2. Visit the root
3. Visit the right sub tree in order

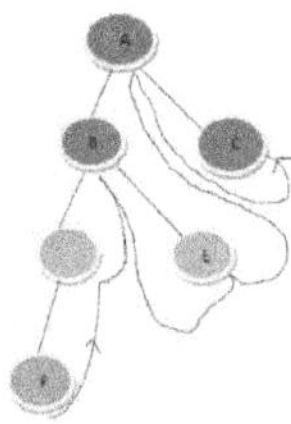

Figure 5.16: In Order Traversal of Left Skewed Binary Tree

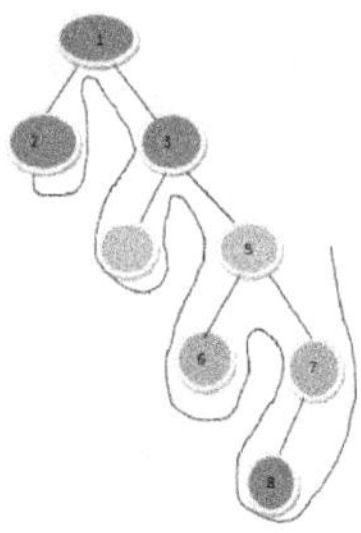

Figure 5.17: In Order Traversal of Right Skewed Binary Tree

In order traversal of T1 is **FDBEAC** and T2 is **21436587.**

Pre Order Tree Traversal Technique: In the pre order tree traversal technique we visit the nodes of a binary tree in the following order:

1. Visit the root
2. Visit the left sub tree in the pre order
3. Visit the right sub tree in the post order

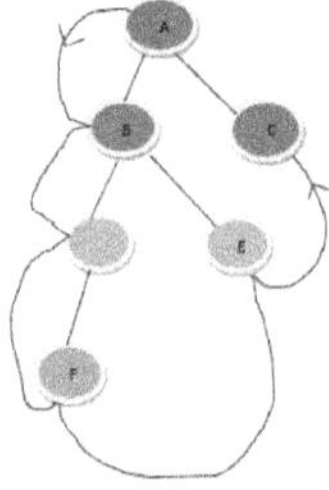

Figure 5.18: Preorder Traversal of Left Skewed Binary Tree

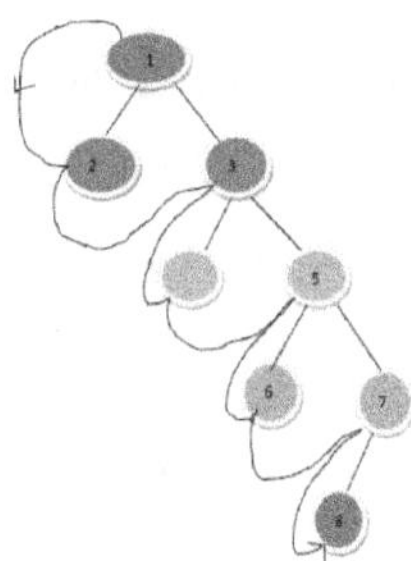

Figure 5.19: Preorder Traversal of Right Skewed Binary Tree

Pre order traversal of T3 is ABDFEC and T4 is 12345678.

Post Order Tree Traversal Technique: In the post order tree traversal technique we will visit all the nodes in the following order:

1. Visit the left sub tree in the pre order
2. Visit the right sub tree in the post order
3. Visit the root

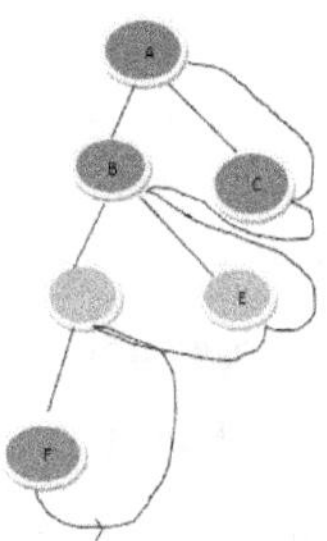

Figure 5.20: Post Order Traversal of Left Skewed Binary Tree

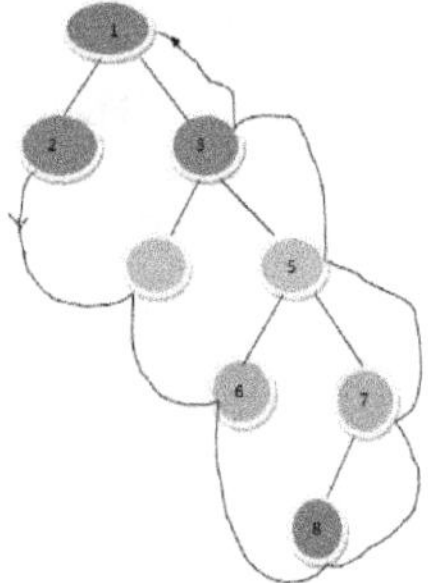

Figure 5.21: Post Order Traversal of Right Skewed Binary Tree

Post order traversal of the T5 is FDEBCA and T6 is 24687531.

Level order tree traversal technique: In the level order tree traversal technique we visit the vertices or nodes in the order of their level from top to bottom.

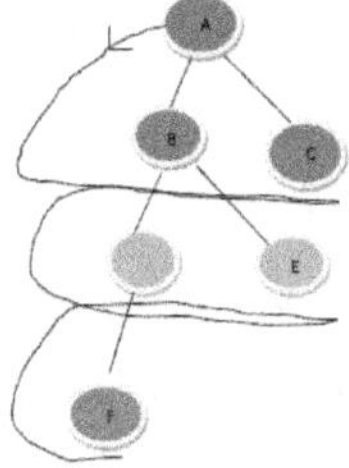

Figure 5.22: Level Order Traversal of Left Skewed Binary Tree

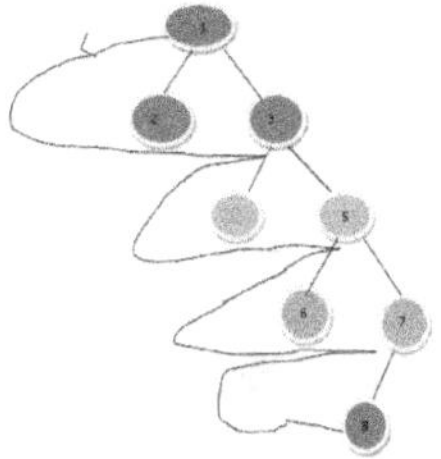

Figure 5.23: Level Order Traversal of Right Skewed Binary Tree

Level order tree traversal of T7 is ABCDEF and T8 is 12345678.

Exercise 1: Find the in order, pre order, post order and level wise traversal of the given binary trees.

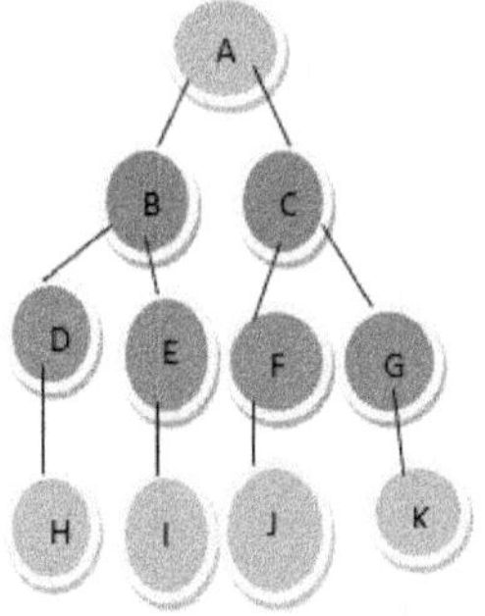

Figure 5.24: Binary Tree for Exercise

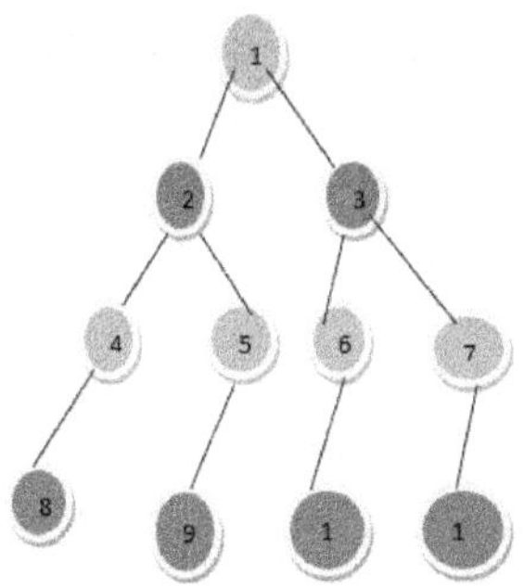

Figure 5.25: Binary Tree for Exercise

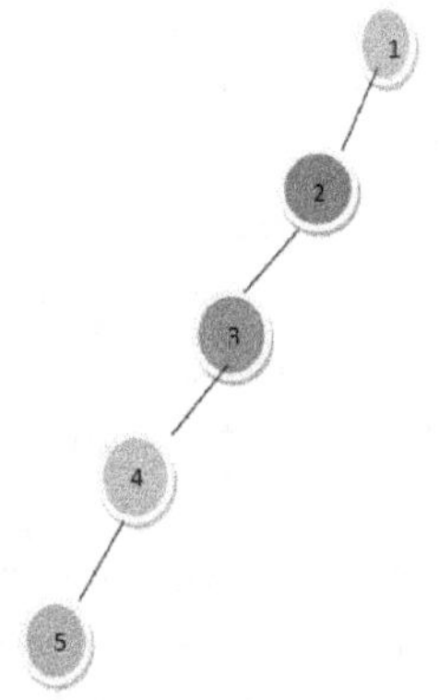

Figure 5.26: Binary Tree for Exercise

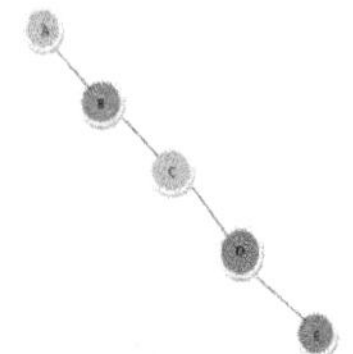

Figure 5.27: Binary Tree for Exercise

5.1.4. Binary Search Trees

A binary search tree is a nonlinear data structure in which elements in the left sub tree are less than or equal to the root and the elements in the right sub tree are always greater than or equal to the root. Binary search trees are actually constructed to speed up search operation. In the best case we require O (1) time to find the element, in the average and worst cases it takes O (h) and O (n) respectively. Where h represents the height and n represents the no of nodes in a binary search tree. The specialty of the BST is that if we traverse the BST in the in order, we get the elements in the ascending order.

Example:

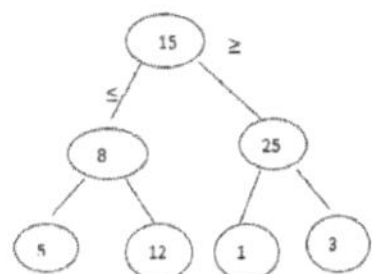

Figure 5.28: Binary Search Tree

Most common operations performed on the BST are:

1. Search

2. Insertion

3. Delete

Search Operation: Search operation is performed on the BST to know whether that element is available in the BST or not. When we look for some element in the binary search tree we generally start searching for that element from the root. If the search element is not the root, we will see whether the element is greater than the root or not. If it is greater than the root, we continue our search operation in the right sub tree recursively till that element is found or the sub tree is exhausted. Otherwise means if the search element is less than the root then we continue our search process in the left sub tree recursively till the element is found or the sub tree is exhausted.

Insertion Operation: To insert some element in to the BST we always compare that element with the root. If the new element is greater than the root, we insert that element in the right sub tree at leaf level as a leaf otherwise we insert that element in the left sub tree at the leaf level as a leaf.

Example: Assume we have been given a binary search tree T as follows. And we are requested to insert elements 13 and 20 to the given BST.

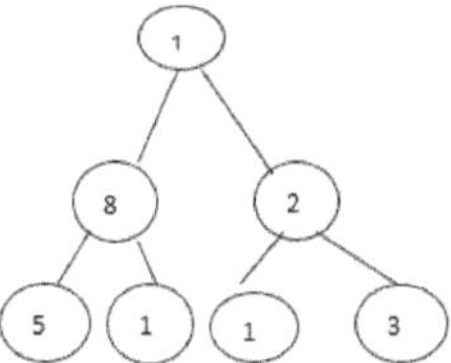

Figure 5.29: Binary Search Tree T

Sol: First of all, let us try to insert the element 13 into the above BST. To insert 13 into the BST first we have to compare that with the root. It is not equal to the root then we will see whether it is less than the root or not. Yes, it is less than the root so we should insert that element in the left sub tree at the leaf level as a leaf. So, in the next level we compare it with the element 8 because it is the root of the left sub tree. Here it is greater than 8. So, we jump into the right sub tree. In the present right sub tree, there is only one element that is 12. So, it should be inserted as the child of the node 12. Here an important question is whether it should be inserted as the left child or the right child so for which again we have to compare it with the 12. Where, 13 is greater than the 12 so, we have to insert that element as a right child of 12. Below figure shows the BST after insertion of 13.

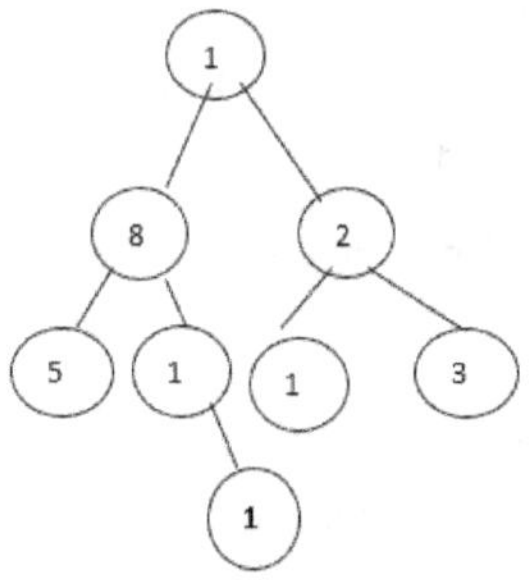

Figure 5.30: Binary Search Tree T After Insertion of 12

Next element to be inserted is 20. The element to be inserted is compared with the root, here 20 is not equal to the root 15. So, we will see whether it is less than the root but it is not less than the root so it is greater than the root. Means we have to insert the element in the right sub tree. In the next step after jumping into the right sub tree we compare it with the element 25. Here it is not equal to 25. Then we will verify whether it is less than 25 or not. Yes, it is less than 25 so we jump into the left sub tree of the element 25. In the left sub tree, we have only one element i.e. 18, so we check whether it is equal to or less than or greater than 18. As the element 20 is greater than 18, we insert element 29 as the right child. The BST after inserting the element 20 is as follows.

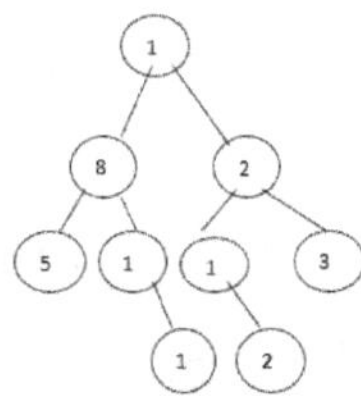

Figure 5.31: Binary Search Tree T After Insertion of 20

Delete Operation: To delete some element from the BST, first of all we should verify whether that element is present in the BST or not. If it is there then we can think or removing that element otherwise we can't remove that element from the BST. If it is there in the BST then to remove that element from the BST, we will do the following things.

1. If the element we wish to remove is the root then replace it with the in-order successor of it.
2. If the element we want to remove is the internal element then to remove it we replace it with the in-order successor of it.
3. If the element we wish to remove is a leaf then simply remove it.

Advantages of BST: Search, insert and delete operations can be done easily.

Disadvantages of BST: It takes more time if the BST is a skewed tree.

Applications of BST:

1. It is used by the memory allocators (Ex: operating System) for allocating the memory.
2. It is used in the Best fit memory allocation algorithm.

Note: We should always try to keep the BST as balanced binary tree.

Ex: AVL tree, Red & Black tree and Splay tree.

5.1.5. AVL Tree

An AVL tree is self-height balanced binary search tree in which the height difference between the left sub tree and right sub tree is at most differed by 1. AVL tree is developed by **A**delson **V**elski **L**andid so it is named as AVL.

Examples:

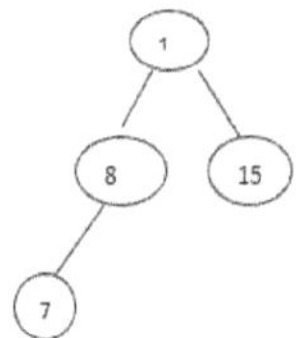

Figure 5.32: AVL Tree T

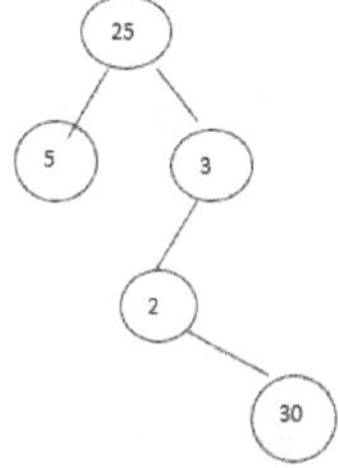

Figure 5.33: AVL Tree T

In the above figures a1 is an AVL tree and a2 is not an AVL tree.

If the height difference between the left sub tree and right sub tree is greater than one then tree is balanced using some rotations. They are as follows:

1. Left rotation
2. Right rotation
3. Left Right rotation
4. Right Left rotation

Left Rotation: A left rotation is required if the BST is right heavy tree. A right heavy tree means the height of the right sub tree is more than the left sub tree. Example for right heavy BST is R1. To know whether a BST is right heavy or not we calculate the balance factor. The balance factor is calculated as follows:

Balance factor = height of the right sub tree – height of the left sub tree.

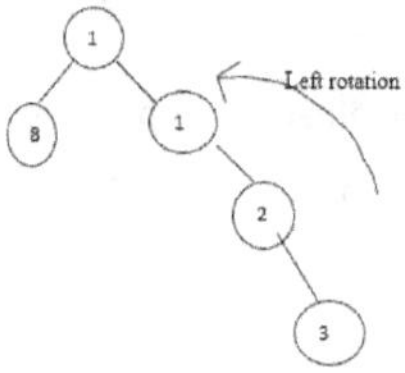

Figure 5.34: Right Skewed AVL Tree

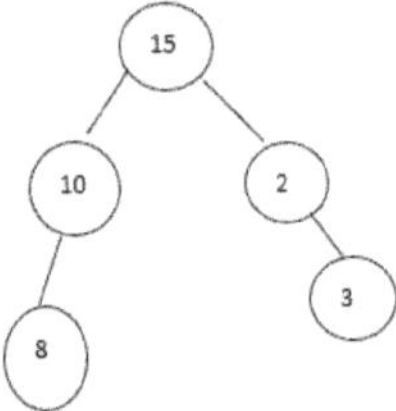

Figure 5.35: Right Skewed AVL Tree After Left Rotation

As the tree R1 is right heavy BST we need to perform a left rotation. The resultant BST after left rotation we can see in the figure R2.

Right Rotation: A right rotation is required when the given tree is left heavy. A left heavy tree is a BST in which the height of the left sub tree is more than the right sub tree. To know whether the tree is left heavy or not we calculate the balance factor. If the balance factor of any node is less than -1, we can assume that the tree is a left heavy tree. In such situations we perform right rotation on the node where the balance factor is less than -1to make the tree balanced.

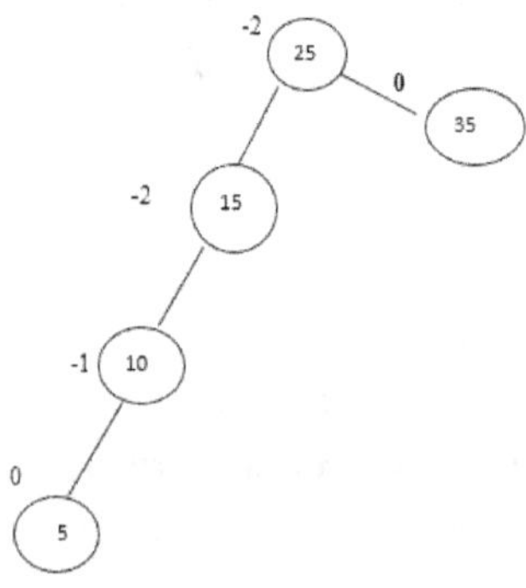

Figure 5.36: (UN Balanced AVL Tree)

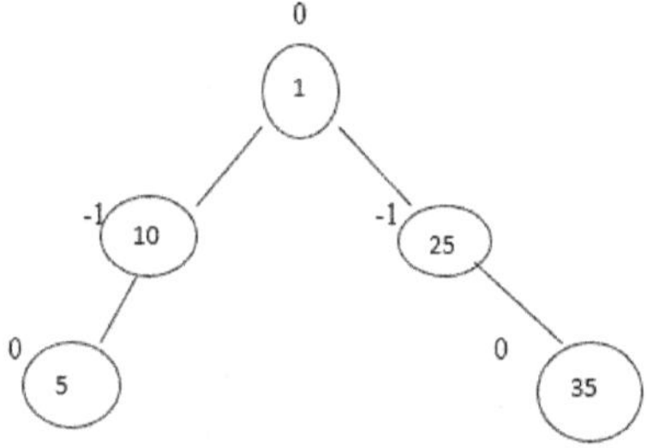

Figure 5.37: (Balanced AVL Tree)

Left Right Rotation: It is a combination of left rotation followed by a right rotation. If the balance of the AVL tree is disturbed by inserting some element in the left sub tree as a right child then we to perform a left rotation followed by a right rotation.

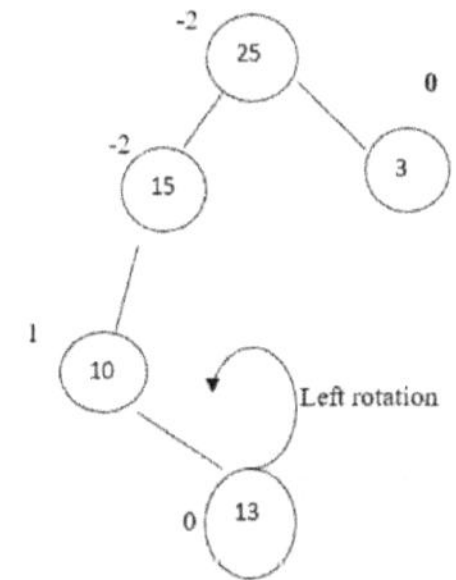

Figure 5.38: Left Rotation on AVL

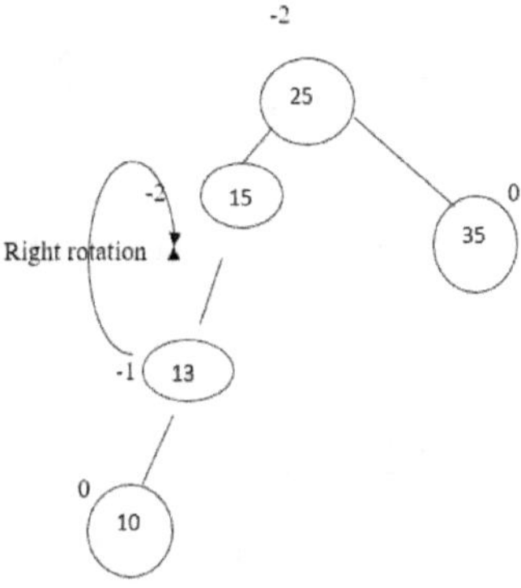

Figure 5.39: Right Rotation on AVL

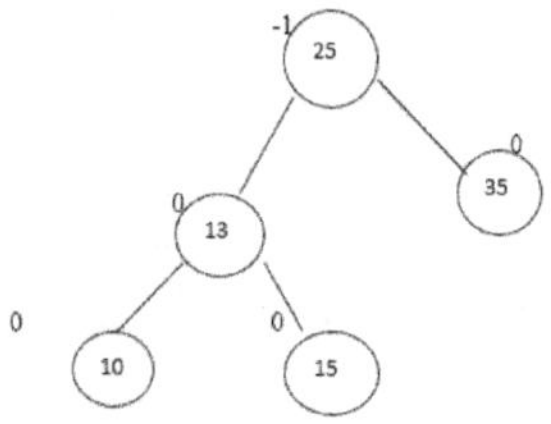

Figure 5.40: Balanced AVL Tree After Left Right Rotation

Right Left Rotation: In right left rotation we perform right rotation followed by left rotation. Right left rotation is required when we insert some element in the right sub tree as a left child and assume because of this insertion the height of the AVL tree is disturbed.

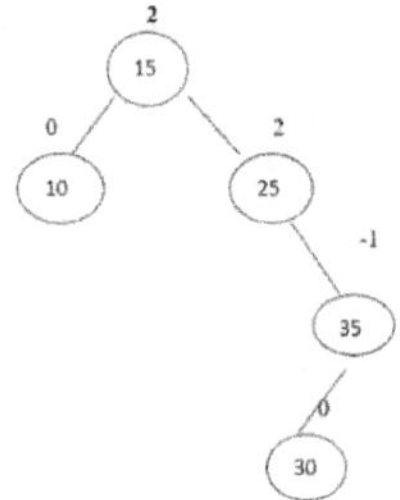

Figure 5.41: Right Left Heavy AVL Tree

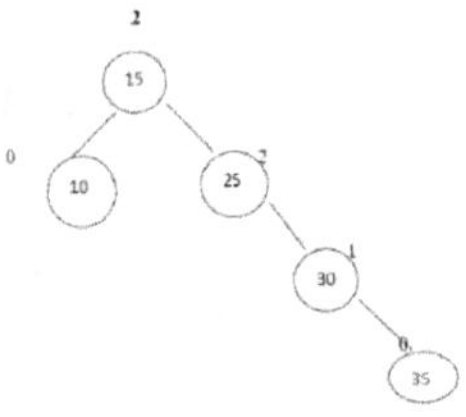

Figure 5.42: After Right Rotation on AVL Tree

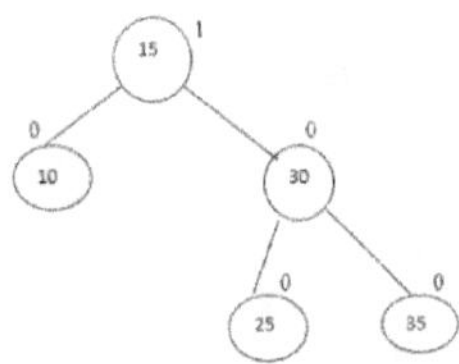

Figure 5.43: After Left Rotation on AVL Tree

5.1.6. Red and Black Tree

Red and black tree is a self-balanced binary search tree similar to AVL tree. The worst-case time complexity for insertion, deletion, and search operations of red and black tree is equal to the AVL tree, i.e. O (logn). Though the worst-case time complexity is equal to the AVL tree people generally won't prefer AVL tree because it takes too many rotations compared with red and black tree. As rotation is more time consuming or costly job than any other job, we prefer red and black tree over AVL tree.

A red and black tree will have following properties:

1. Each and every node in the red and black tree should be colored either with red or black color.
2. Root should be always colored in black.
3. No two adjacent nodes should the red color.
4. Back height of each path should be equal. Black height is nothing but the no of black nodes in each path.
5. Height of the red and black tree is always restricted to O(log n).

    Red and black trees are used in the applications where insertion and deletion operations are performed so frequently. If search operation is performed so frequently, we prefer AVL tree rather than the red and black tree.

Insertion Operation: Insertion operation in the red and black tree is similar to the insertion operation in the binary search tree means the new elements are inserted in the leaf level as a leaf only. The newly inserted element color is always red. If it is the first element or node in the red and black tree then its color is changed to black. If the newly inserted node's uncle color is red then the parent and its uncle color is changed to black otherwise a rotation is performed.

1. If the newly inserted element is the root then change its color to black.
2. If the newly inserted element is not the root or its color is not black then do the following.
    a) If x's uncle color is red then change the color of its parent and uncle to black.
    b) Change the color of its grandparent to red. Now assume grandparent as x and repeat step1 and step2.
3. If x's parent is black then there are three possibilities.
    a) **Left Left Case:** If x is the left child of p and p is the left child of grandparent then a right rotation is performed and parent and grandparent colors are swapped.

b) Right Right Case: If x is the right child of p and p is the right child of its grandparent then a left rotation is performed followed a swap of colors of parent and grandparent.

c) Left Right Case: if x is the left child of p and p is the right child of its grandparent g then a left rotation is performed followed by a right rotation. And swap the colors of parent and grandparent colors.

d) Right Left Case: if x is the right child of p and p is the left child of its grandparent g then a right rotation is performed followed by a left rotation. And swap the colors of the parent and grandparent.

Example: Consider the following example to demonstrate the insertion operation in the red and black tree.

Let us assume x is the newly inserted element and y is the uncle of x.

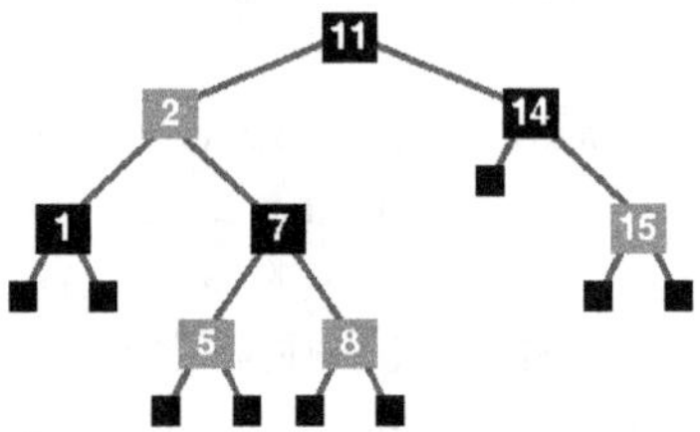

Figure 5.44: Red and Black Tree

In the above the black sentinel nodes have been omitted for the simplification.

Insert element 4 as the left child of the element 5. After the element 4 is inserted the above red and black tree will be disturbed and we can't call it as a red and black tree because 4 and 5 coloreds in red.

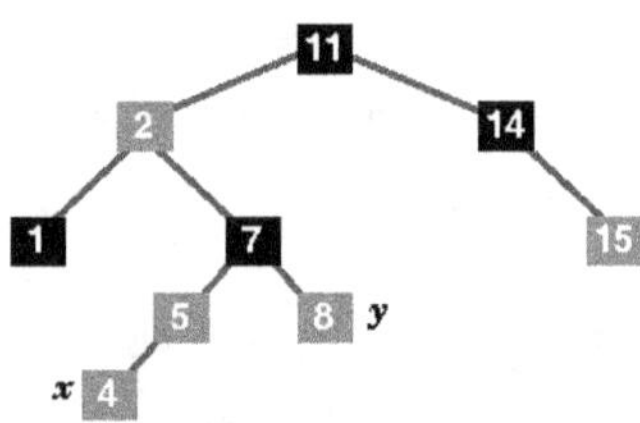

Figure 5.45: Red and Black Tree After Insertion of X and Y

When new element 4 is inserted as a left child of element 5 then the parent and child colors are matched. So, we try to change the color of 5 and 8 to black and 7 color as red. The resultant red and black tree will be as follows.

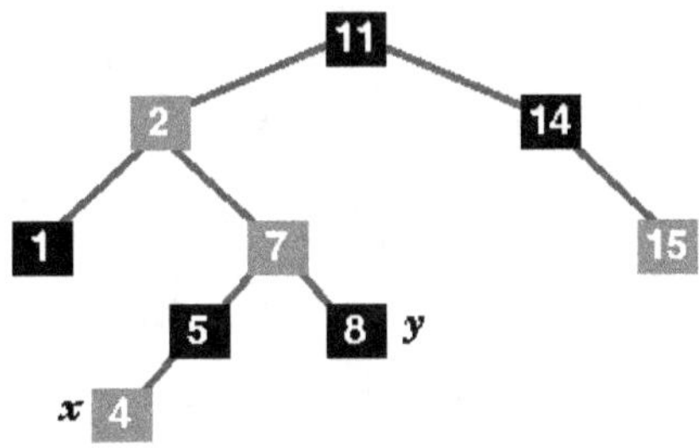

Figure 5.46: Red and Black Tree After Colour Adjustment

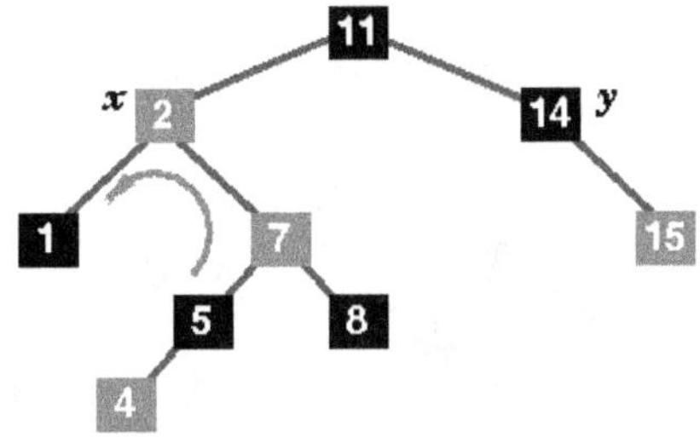

Figure 5.47: Red and Black Tree Needs Left Rotation

At this point the present red and black tree looks unbalanced so to make the tree as balanced we need to perform a left rotation at element 2. The resultant red and black tree is as follows.

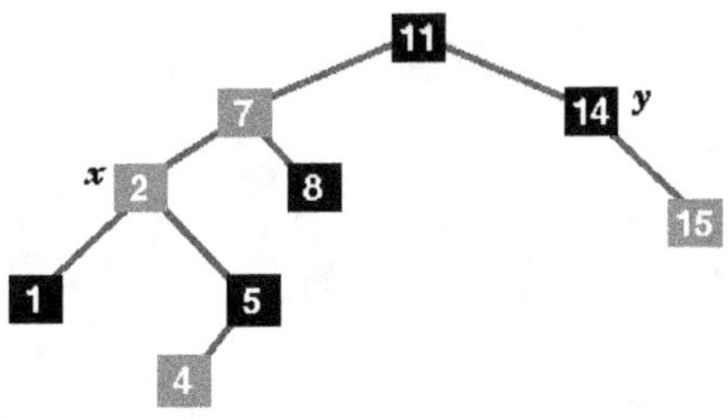

Figure 5.48: Red and Black Tree After Left Rotation

Still the tree is not a red and black tree because uncle is black and parent is red so we change the color of 7 into black. Even after changing the color of 7 into black, the tree is not a red and black tree because it is not satisfying the black height property of it. Consider the figure R7. To make the tree as a height balanced red and black tree, we need to perform a right rotation at element 7. The resultant red and black is as shown in the figure R9. The result of the rotation gives us a balanced red and black tree with height O(logn).

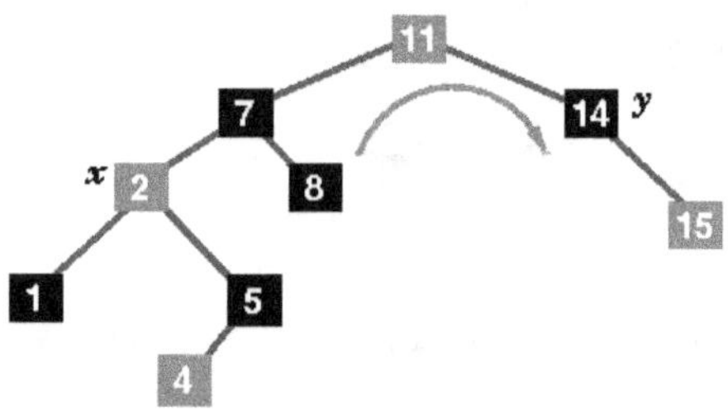

Figure 5.49: Red and Black Tree Needs Right Rotation

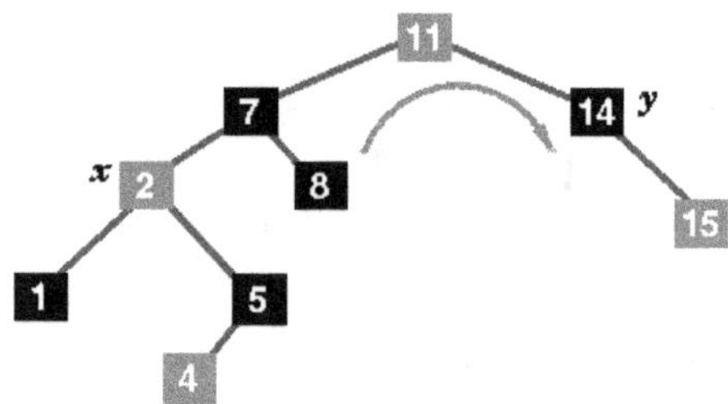

Figure 5.50: Red and Black Tree Needs Left Rotation

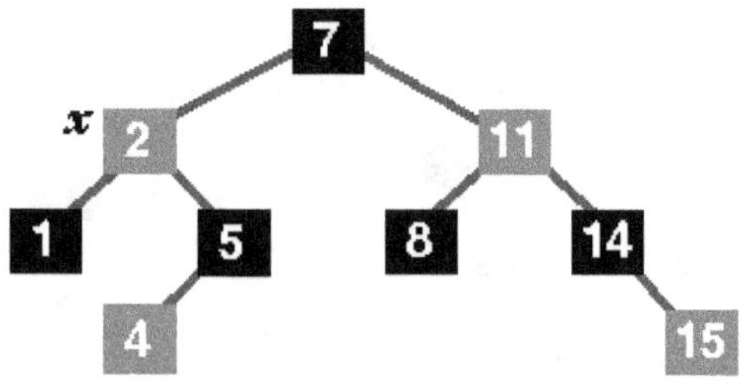

Figure 5.51: Height Balanced Red and Black Tree

```cpp
#include <iostream>
#include <queue>
using namespace std;

enum COLOR {RED, BLACK};

class Node {
public:
  int val;
  COLOR color;
  Node *left, *right, *parent;

  Node(int val): val(val) {
    parent = left = right = NULL;

    // Node is created during insertion
    // Node is red at insertion
    color = RED;
  }

  // returns pointer to uncle
  Node *uncle() {
    // If no parent or grandparent, then no uncle
    if (parent == NULL or parent->parent == NULL)
      return NULL;

    if (parent->isOnLeft())
      // uncle on right
      return parent->parent->right;
    else
      // uncle on left
      return parent->parent->left;
  }
```

```cpp
  // check if node is left child of parent
  bool isOnLeft() {return this == parent->left;}

  // returns pointer to sibling
  Node *sibling() {
    // sibling null if no parent
    if (parent == NULL)
      return NULL;

    if (isOnLeft())
      return parent->right;

    return parent->left;
  }

  // moves node down and moves given node in its place
  void moveDown(Node *nParent) {
    if (parent! = NULL) {
      if (is On Left ()) {
        parent->left = nParent;
      } else {
        parent->right = nParent;
      }
    }
    nParent->parent = parent;
    parent = nParent;
  }
  bool has Red Child() {
  return (left! = NULL and left->color == RED) or
      (right! = NULL and right->color == RED);
  }
};

class RBTree {
```

```cpp
Node *root;

// left rotates the given node
void leftRotate(Node *x) {
  // new parent will be node's right child
  Node *nParent = x->right;

  // update root if current node is root
  if (x == root)
    root = nParent;

  x->moveDown(nParent);

  // connect x with new parent's left element
  x->right = nParent->left;
  // connect new parent's left element with node
  // if it is not null
  if (nParent->left! = NULL)
    nParent->left->parent = x;

  // connect new parent with x
  nParent->left = x;
}

void rightRotate (Node *x) {
  // new parent will be node's left child
  Node *nParent = x->left;
  // update root if current node is root
  if (x == root)
    root = nParent;

  x->move Down(nParent);

  // connect x with new parent's right element
```

```c
  x->left = nParent->right;
  // connect new parent's right element with node
  // if it is not null
  if (nParent-> right! = NULL)
    nParent->right->parent = x;

  // connect new parent with x
  nParent->right = x;
}


void swapColors (Node *x1, Node *x2) {
  COLOR temp;
  temp = x1->color;
  x1->color = x2->color;
  x2->color = temp;
}


void swapValues(Node *u, Node *v) {
  int temp;
  temp = u->val;
  u->val = v->val;
  v->val = temp;
}


// fix red red at given node
void fixRedRed(Node *x) {
  // if x is root color it black and return
  if (x == root) {
    x->color = BLACK;
    return;
  }

  // initialize parent, grandparent, uncle
  Node *parent = x->parent, *grandparent = parent->parent,
```

```cpp
  *uncle = x->uncle();

if (parent->color! = BLACK) {
  if (uncle! = NULL && uncle->color == RED) {
    // uncle red, perform recoloring and recurse
    parent->color = BLACK;
    uncle->color = BLACK;
    grandparent->color = RED;
    fixRedRed(grandparent);
  } else {
    // Else perform LR, LL, RL, RR
    if (parent->isOnLeft()) {
     if (x->isOnLeft()) {
       // for left right
       swapColors(parent, grandparent);
     } else {
       leftRotate(parent);
       swapColors (x, grandparent);
     }
     // for left left and left right
     rightRotate(grandparent);
    } else {
     if (x->isOnLeft()) {
       // for right left
       rightRotate(parent);
       swapColors(x, grandparent);
     } else {
       swapColors(parent, grandparent);
     }

     // for right right and right left
     leftRotate(grandparent);
    }
  }
```

```cpp
  }
}

// find node that do not have a left child
// in the subtree of the given node
Node *successor(Node *x) {
  Node *temp = x;

  while (temp->left! = NULL)
    temp = temp->left;

  return temp;
}

// find node that replaces a deleted node in BST
Node *BSTreplace (Node *x) {
  // when node have 2 children
  if (x->left! = NULL and x->right != NULL)
    return successor(x->right);

  // when leaf
  if (x->left == NULL and x->right == NULL)
    return NULL;

  // when single child
  if (x->left! = NULL)
    return x->left;
  else
    return x->right;
}

// deletes the given node
void deleteNode(Node *v) {
  Node *u = BSTreplace(v);
```

```cpp
  // True when u and v are both black
  bool uvBlack = ((u == NULL or u->color == BLACK) and (v->color == BLACK));
  Node *parent = v->parent;

  if (u == NULL) {
    // u is NULL therefore v is leaf
    if (v == root) {
      // v is root, making root null
      root = NULL;
    } else {
      if (uvBlack) {
        // u and v both black
        // v is leaf, fix double black at v
        fixDoubleBlack(v);
      } else {
        // u or v is red
        if (v->sibling()! = NULL)
          // sibling is not null, make it red"
          v->sibling()->color = RED;
      }

      // delete v from the tree
      if (v->isOnLeft()) {
        parent->left = NULL;
      } else {
        parent->right = NULL;
      }
    }
    delete v;
    return;
  }

  if (v->left == NULL or v->right == NULL) {
    // v has 1 child
```

```cpp
  if (v == root) {
    // v is root, assign the value of u to v, and delete u
    v->val = u->val;
    v->left = v->right = NULL;
    delete u;
  } else {
    // Detach v from tree and move u up
    if (v->isOnLeft()) {
      parent->left = u;
    } else {
      parent->right = u;
    }
    delete v;
    u->parent = parent;
    if (uvBlack) {
      // u and v both black, fix double black at u
      fixDoubleBlack(u);
    } else {
      // u or v red, color u black
      u->color = BLACK;
    }
  }
  return;
}


// v has 2 children, swap values with successor and recurse
swapValues (u, v);
deleteNode (u);
}


void fixDoubleBlack(Node *x) {
if (x == root)
  // Reached root
  return;
```

```cpp
 Node *sibling = x->sibling(), *parent = x->parent;
if (sibling == NULL) {
  // No sibiling, double black pushed up
  fixDoubleBlack(parent);
} else {
  if (sibling->color == RED) {
    // Sibling red
    parent->color = RED;
    sibling->color = BLACK;
    if (sibling->isOnLeft()) {
      // left case
      rightRotate(parent);
    } else {
      // right case
      leftRotate(parent);
    }
    fixDoubleBlack(x);
  } else {
    // Sibling black
    if (sibling->hasRedChild()) {
      // at least 1 red children
      if (sibling->left! = NULL and sibling->left->color == RED) {
        if (sibling->isOnLeft()) {
          // left left
          sibling->left->color = sibling->color;
          sibling->color = parent->color;
          rightRotate(parent);
        } else {
          // right left
          sibling->left->color = parent->color;
          rightRotate(sibling);
          leftRotate(parent);
        }
      } else {
```

```cpp
      if (sibling->isOnLeft()) {
        // leftright
        sibling->right->color = parent->color;
        leftRotate(sibling);
        rightRotate(parent);
      } else {
        // right right
        sibling->right->color = sibling->color;
        sibling->color = parent->color;
        leftRotate(parent);
      }
    }
    parent->color = BLACK;
  } else {
    // 2 black children
    sibling->color = RED;
    if (parent->color == BLACK)
      fixDoubleBlack(parent);
    else
      parent->color = BLACK;
  }
  }
 }
}

// prints level order for given node
void levelOrder(Node *x) {
  if (x == NULL)
    // return if node is null
    return;

  // queue for level order
  queue<Node *> q;
  Node *curr;
```

```cpp
    // push x
    q. push (x);

    while (! q. empty ()) {
      // while q is not empty
      // dequeue
      curr = q.front();
      q.pop();

      // print node value
      cout << curr->val << " ";

      // push children to queue
      if (curr->left! = NULL)
        q. push (curr->left);
      if (curr->right! = NULL)
        q. push (curr->right);
    }
  }

  // prints inorder recursively
  void inorder (Node *x) {
    if (x == NULL)
      return;
    inorder(x->left);
    cout << x->val << " ";
    inorder(x->right);
  }

public:
  // constructor
  // initialize root
  RBTree() {root = NULL;}
  Node *getRoot() {g return root;}
```

```cpp
// searches for given value
// if found returns the node (used for delete)
// else returns the last node while traversing (used in insert)
Node *search(int n) {
  Node *temp = root;
  while (temp! = NULL) {
    if (n < temp->val) {
      if (temp->left == NULL)
        break;
      else
        temp = temp->left;
    } else if (n == temp->val) {
      break;
    } else {
      if (temp->right == NULL)
        break;
      else
        temp = temp->right;
    }
  }

  return temp;
}

// inserts the given value to tree
void insert(int n) {
  Node *newNode = new Node(n);
  if (root == NULL) {
    // when root is null
    // simply insert value at root
    newNode->color = BLACK;
    root = newNode;
  } else {
    Node *temp = search(n);
```

```cpp
    if (temp->val == n) {
      // return if value already exists
      return;
    }


    // if value is not found, search returns the node
    // where the value is to be inserted

    // connect new node to correct node
    newNode->parent = temp;

    if (n < temp->val)
      temp->left = newNode;
    else
      temp->right = newNode;

    // fix red red voilaton if exists
    fixRedRed(newNode);
   }
 }


// utility function that deletes the node with given value
void deleteByVal(int n) {
  if (root == NULL)
    // Tree is empty
    return;

  Node *v = search(n), *u;

  if (v->val! = n) {
    cout << "No node found to delete with value:" << n << endl;
    return;
  }
  deleteNode(v);
```

```cpp
}

  // prints inorder of the tree
  void printInOrder() {
    cout << "Inorder: " << endl;
    if (root == NULL)
      cout << "Tree is empty" << endl;
    else
      inorder(root);
    cout << endl;
  }

  // prints level order of the tree
  void printLevelOrder() {
    cout << "Level order: " << endl;
    if (root == NULL)
      cout << "Tree is empty" << endl;
    else
      levelOrder(root);
    cout << endl;
  }
};

int main() {
  RBTree tree;

  tree. insert(7);
  tree. insert(3);
  tree. insert(18);
  tree. insert(10);
  tree. insert(22);
  tree. insert(8);
  tree. insert(11);
  tree. insert(26);
```

```cpp
    tree. insert(2);
    tree. insert(6);
    tree. insert(13);

    tree. printInOrder();
    tree. printLevelOrder();

    cout<<endl<<"Deleting 18, 11, 3, 10, 22"<<endl;

    tree. deleteByVal(18);
    tree. deleteByVal(11);
    tree. deleteByVal(3);
    tree. deleteByVal(10);
    tree. deleteByVal(22);

    tree. printInOrder();
    tree. printLevelOrder();
    return 0;
}
```

Insertion Vs Deletion

Like Insertion, re coloring and rotations are used to maintain the Red-Black properties. In insert operation, we check color of uncle to decide the appropriate case. In delete operation, **we check color of sibling** to decide the appropriate case.

The main property that violates after insertion is two consecutive reds. In delete, the main violated property is, change of black height in sub trees as deletion of a black node may cause reduced black height in one root to leaf path.

Deletion is fairly complex process. To understand deletion, notion of double black is used. When a black node is deleted and replaced by a black child, the child is marked as **double black**. The main task now becomes to convert this double black to single black.

Deletion Steps

The following are detailed steps for deletion.

1) Perform standard BST delete. When we perform standard delete operation in BST, we always end up deleting a node which is either leaf or has only one child (For an internal node, we copy the successor and then recursively call delete for successor, successor is always a leaf node or a node with one child). So we only need to handle cases where a node is leaf or has one child. Let v be the node to be deleted and u be the child that replaces v (Note that u is NULL when v is a leaf and color of NULL is considered as Black).

2) Simple Case: If either u or v is red, we mark the replaced child as black (No change in black height). Note that both u and v cannot be red as v is parent of u and two consecutive reds are not allowed in red-black tree.

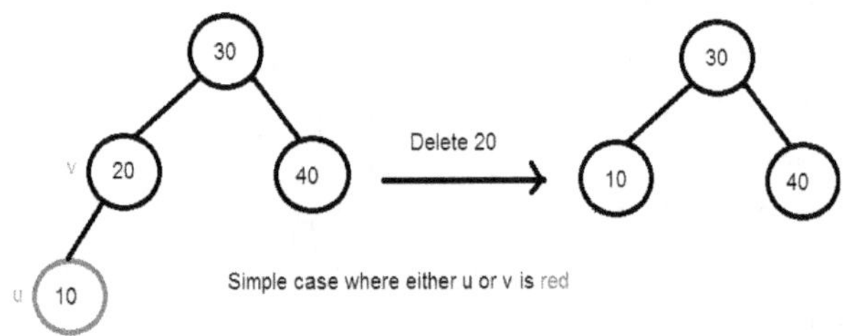

Figure 5.52: Delete Operation Over Red and Black Tree

3) If both u and v are Black

3.1) Color u as double black. Now our task reduces to, convert this double black to single black. Note that If v is leaf, then u is NULL and color of NULL is considered as black. So the deletion of a black leaf also causes a double black.

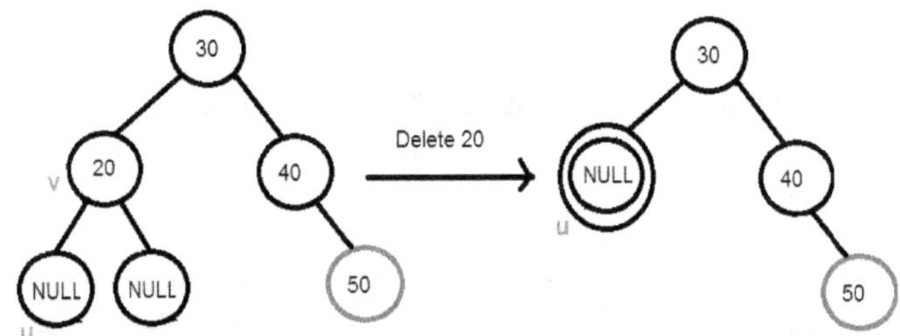

Figure 5.53: Delete Operation Over Red and Black Tree

3.2) Do following while the current node u is double black and it is not root? Let sibling of node be **s**.

(a): If sibling s is black and at least one of sibling's children is red, perform rotation(s). Let the red child of s be **r**. This case can be divided into four sub cases depending upon position of s and r.

(i) Left Left Case (s is left child of its parent and r is left child of s or both children of s are red). This is mirror of right right case shown in below diagram.

(ii) Left Right Case (s is left child of its parent and r is right child). This is mirror of right left case shown in below diagram.

(iii) Right Right Case (s is right child of its parent and r is right child of s or both children of s are red).

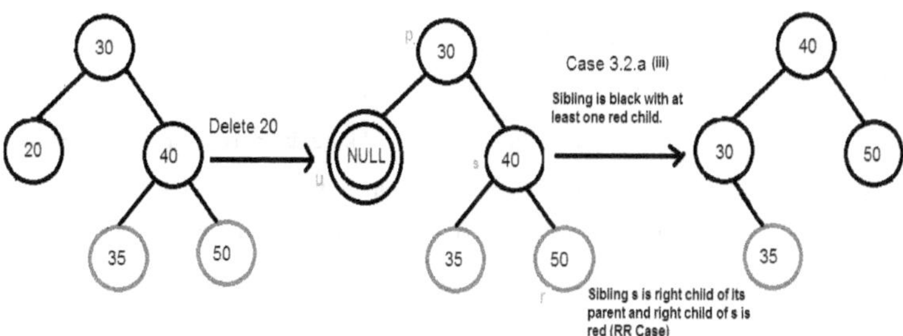

Figure 5.54: Delete Operation Over Red and Black Tree

iv) Right Left Case (s is right child of its parent and r is left child of s).

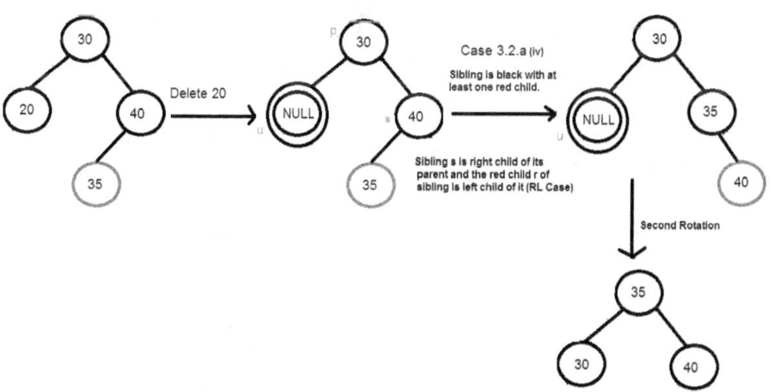

Figure 5.55: Balanced Red and Black Tree

(b): If sibling is black and it's both children are black. Perform re coloring and recur for the parent if parent is black.

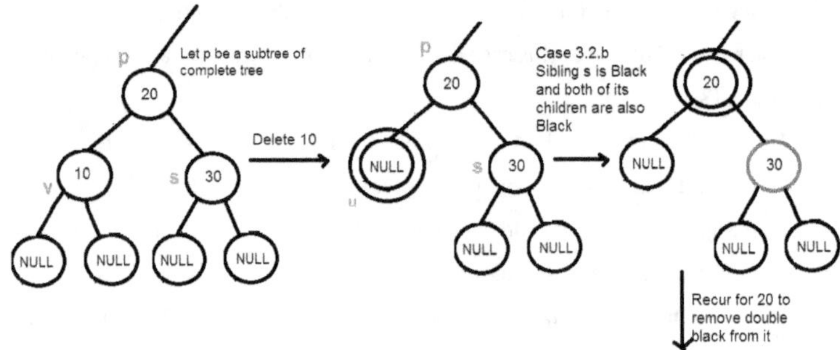

Figure 5.56: Delete 10 from Red and Black Tree

In this case, if parent was red, then we didn't need to recur for present, we can simply make it black (red + double black =single black).

(c): If sibling is red: Perform a rotation to move old sibling up, recolor the old sibling and parent. The new sibling is always black. This mainly converts the tree to black sibling case and leads to case a or b. This case can be divided in two sub cases.

i)   Left Case (s is left child of its parent). This is mirror of right right case shown in below diagram. We right rotate the parent p.

ii) Right case (s is the right child of its parent). We left rotate the parent p.

iii) Right left case (s is right child of its parent and r is left child of s).

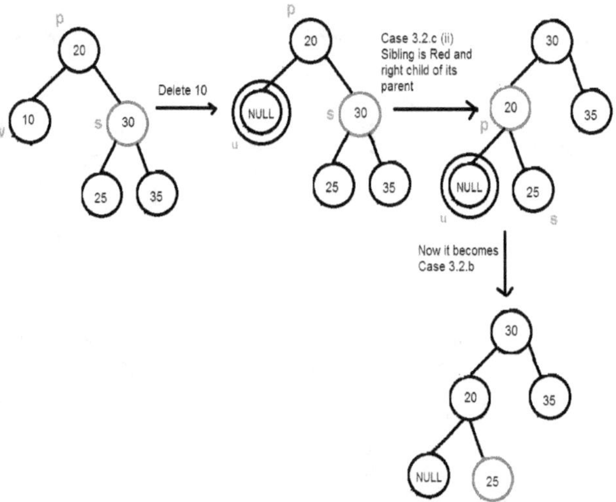

Figure 5.57: Balanced Red and Black Tree After Deleting 10

(d): If sibling is red, perform a rotation to move old sibling up, recolor the old sibling and parent. The new sibling is always black (See the below diagram). This mainly converts the tree to black sibling case (by rotation) and leads to case (a) or (b). This case can be divided in two sub cases:

    (i) Left Case (s is left child of its parent). This is mirror of right right case shown in below diagram. We right rotate the parent p.

    (iii) Right Case (s is right child of its parent). We left rotate the parent p.

3.3) If u is root make it single black and return

```cpp
#include <iostream>
#include <queue>
using namespace std;


enum COLOR {RED, BLACK};


class Node {
public:
int val;
COLOR color;
Node *left, *right, *parent;

Node(int val): val(val) {
parent = left = right = NULL;

// Node is created during insertion
// Node is red at insertion
color = RED;
}


// returns pointer to uncle
Node *uncle() {
// If no parent or grandparent, then no uncle
if (parent == NULL or parent->parent == NULL)
return NULL;
```

```cpp
if (parent->isOnLeft())
// uncle on right
return parent->parent->right;
else
// uncle on left
return parent->parent->left;
}

// check if node is left child of parent
bool isOnLeft() {return this == parent->left;}

// returns pointer to sibling
Node *sibling() {
// sibling null if no parent
if (parent == NULL)
return NULL;

if (isOnLeft())
return parent->right;

return parent->left;
}

// moves node down and moves given node in its place
void moveDown(Node *nParent) {
if (parent! = NULL) {
if (isOnLeft()) {
parent->left = nParent;
} else {
parent->right = nParent;
}
}
```

```cpp
nParent->parent = parent;
parent = nParent;
}

bool hasRedChild() {
return (left! = NULL and left->color == RED) or
(right! = NULL and right->color == RED);
}
};

class RBTree {
Node *root;

// left rotates the given node
void leftRotate (Node *x) {
// new parent will be node's right child
Node *nParent = x->right;

// update root if current node is root
if (x == root)
root = nParent;

x->moveDown(nParent);

// connect x with new parent's left element
x->right = nParent->left;
// connect new parent's left element with node
// if it is not null
if (nParent->left! = NULL)
nParent->left->parent = x;

// connect new parent with x
nParent->left = x;
```

```cpp
}

void rightRotate (Node *x) {
// new parent will be node's left child
Node *nParent = x->left;

// update root if current node is root
if (x == root)
root = nParent;

x->moveDown(nParent);

// connect x with new parent's right element
x->left = nParent->right;
// connect new parent's right element with node
// if it is not null
if (nParent->right! = NULL)
nParent->right->parent = x;

// connect new parent with x
nParent->right = x;
}

void swapColors (Node *x1, Node *x2) {
COLOR temp;
temp = x1->color;
x1->color = x2->color;
x2->color = temp;
}

void swapValues(Node *u, Node *v) {
int temp;
temp = u->val;
```

```cpp
  u->val = v->val;
  v->val = temp;
}

// fix red red at given node
void fixRedRed(Node *x) {
// if x is root color it black and return
if (x == root) {
x->color = BLACK;
return;
}

// initialize parent, grandparent, uncle
Node *parent = x->parent, *grandparent = parent->parent,
*uncle = x->uncle();

if (parent->color! = BLACK) {
if (uncle! = NULL && uncle->color == RED) {
// uncle red, perform recoloring and recurse
parent->color = BLACK;
uncle->color = BLACK;
grandparent->color = RED;
fixRedRed(grandparent);
} else {
// Else perform LR, LL, RL, RR
if (parent->isOnLeft()) {
if (x->isOnLeft()) {
// for left right
swapColors(parent, grandparent);
} else {
leftRotate(parent);
swapColors(x, grandparent);
}
```

```cpp
// for left left and left right
rightRotate (grandparent);
} else {
if (x->isOnLeft()) {
// for right left
rightRotate(parent);
swapColors(x, grandparent);
} else {
swapColors(parent, grandparent);
}

// for right right and right left
leftRotate(grandparent);
}
}
}
}


// find node that do not have a left child
// in the subtree of the given node
Node *successor(Node *x) {
Node *temp = x;

while (temp->left! = NULL)
temp = temp->left;

return temp;
}


// find node that replaces a deleted node in BST
Node *BSTreplace(Node *x) {
// when node have 2 children
if (x->left! = NULL and x->right != NULL)
```

```cpp
return successor(x->right);

// when leaf
if (x->left == NULL and x->right == NULL)
return NULL;

// when single child
if (x->left! = NULL)
return x->left;
else
return x->right;
}

// deletes the given node
void deleteNode(Node *v) {
Node *u = BSTreplace(v);

// True when u and v are both black
bool uvBlack = ((u == NULL or u->color == BLACK) and (v->color == BLACK));
Node *parent = v->parent;

if (u == NULL) {
// u is NULL therefore v is leaf
if (v == root) {
// v is root, making root null
root = NULL;
} else {
if (uvBlack) {
// u and v both black
// v is leaf, fix double black at v
fixDoubleBlack(v);
} else {
// u or v is red
```

```cpp
if (v->sibling()! = NULL)
// sibling is not null, make it red"
v->sibling()->color = RED;
}


// delete v from the tree
if (v->isOnLeft()) {
parent->left = NULL;
} else {
parent->right = NULL;
}
}
delete v;
return;
}


if (v->left == NULL or v->right == NULL) {
// v has 1 child
if (v == root) {
// v is root, assign the value of u to v, and delete u
v->val = u->val;
v->left = v->right = NULL;
delete u;
} else {
// Detach v from tree and move u up
if (v->isOnLeft()) {
parent->left = u;
} else {
parent->right = u;
}
delete v;
u->parent = parent;
if (uvBlack) {
```

```cpp
// u and v both black, fix double black at u
fixDoubleBlack(u);
} else {
// u or v red, color u black
u->color = BLACK;
}
}
return;
}

// v has 2 children, swap values with successor and recurse
swapValues(u, v);
deleteNode(u);
}

void fixDoubleBlack(Node *x) {
if (x == root)
// Reached root
return;

Node *sibling = x->sibling(), *parent = x->parent;
if (sibling == NULL) {
// No sibiling, double black pushed up
fixDoubleBlack(parent);
} else {
if (sibling->color == RED) {
// Sibling red
parent->color = RED;
sibling->color = BLACK;
if (sibling->isOnLeft ()) {
// left case
rightRotate (parent);
} else {
```

```cpp
// right case
leftRotate(parent);
}
fixDoubleBlack(x);
} else {
// Sibling black
if (sibling->hasRedChild()) {
// at least 1 red children
if (sibling->left! = NULL and sibling->left->color == RED) {
if (sibling->isOnLeft()) {
// left left
sibling->left->color = sibling->color;
sibling->color = parent->color;
rightRotate (parent);
} else {
// right left
sibling->left->color = parent->color;
rightRotate(sibling);
leftRotate(parent);
}
} else {
if (sibling->isOnLeft()) {
// left right
sibling->right->color = parent->color;
leftRotate(sibling);
rightRotate(parent);
} else {
// right right
sibling->right->color = sibling->color;
sibling->color = parent->color;
leftRotate(parent);
}
}
```

```cpp
parent->color = BLACK;
} else {
// 2 black children
sibling->color = RED;
if (parent->color == BLACK)
fixDoubleBlack(parent);
else
parent->color = BLACK;
}
}
}
}

// prints level order for given node
void levelOrder(Node *x) {
if (x == NULL)
// return if node is null
return;

// queue for level order
queue<Node *> q;
Node *curr;

// push x
q.push(x);

while (!q.empty()) {
// while q is not empty
// dequeue
curr = q.front();
q.pop();

// print node value
```

```cpp
    cout << curr->val << " ";

    // push children to queue
    if (curr->left! = NULL)
      q. push(curr->left);
    if (curr->right! = NULL)
      q. push(curr->right);
  }
}


// prints inorder recursively
void inorder(Node *x) {
  if (x == NULL)
    return;
  inorder(x->left);
  cout << x->val << " ";
  inorder(x->right);
}


public:
// constructor
// initialize root
RBTree() {root = NULL;}


Node *getRoot() {return root;}


// searches for given value
// if found returns the node (used for delete)
// else returns the last node while traversing (used in insert)
Node *search(int n) {
  Node *temp = root;
  while (temp! = NULL) {
    if (n < temp->val) {
```

```cpp
if (temp->left == NULL)
break;
else
temp = temp->left;
} else if (n == temp->val) {
break;
} else {
if (temp->right == NULL)
break;
else
temp = temp->right;
}
}

return temp;
}

// inserts the given value to tree
void insert(int n) {
Node *newNode = new Node(n);
if (root == NULL) {
// when root is null
// simply insert value at root
newNode->color = BLACK;
root = newNode;
} else {
Node *temp = search(n);

if (temp->val == n) {
// return if value already exists
return;
}
```

```cpp
// if value is not found, search returns the node
// where the value is to be inserted

// connect new node to correct node
newNode->parent = temp;

if (n < temp->val)
temp->left = newNode;
else
temp->right = newNode;

// fix red red voilaton if exists
fixRedRed(newNode);
}
}


// utility function that deletes the node with given value
void deleteByVal(int n) {
if (root == NULL)
// Tree is empty
return;

Node *v = search(n), *u;

if (v->val! = n) {
cout << "No node found to delete with value:" << n << endl;
return;
}
deleteNode(v);
}
// prints inorder of the tree
void printInOrder() {
cout << "Inorder: " << endl;
```

```cpp
if (root == NULL)
cout << "Tree is empty" << endl;
else
inorder(root);
cout << endl;
}
// prints level order of the tree
void printLevelOrder() {
cout << "Level order: " << endl;
if (root == NULL)
cout << "Tree is empty" << endl;
else
levelOrder(root);
cout << endl;
}
};
int main() {
RBTree tree;
tree. insert (7);
tree. insert (3);
tree. insert (18);
tree. insert (10);
tree. insert (22);
tree. insert (8);
tree. insert (11);
tree. insert (26);
tree. insert (2);
tree. insert (6);
tree. insert (13);
tree. printInOrder();
tree. printLevelOrder();
cout<<endl<<"Deleting 18, 11, 3, 10, 22"<<endl;
```

tree. deleteByVal(18);

tree. deleteByVal(11);

tree. deleteByVal(3);

tree. deleteByVal(10);

tree. deleteByVal(22);

tree. printInOrder();

tree. printLevelOrder();

return 0;

}

Output

In order:

2 3 6 7 8 10 11 13 18 22 26

Level order:

10 7 18 3 8 11 22 2 6 13 26

Deleting 18, 11, 3, 10, 22

In order:

2 6 7 8 13 26

Level order:

13 7 26 6 8 2

Differences between AVL Tree and Red and Black Tree

1. AVL trees provide **faster lookups** than Red Black Trees because they are more strictly balanced.

2. Red Black Trees provide **faster insertion and removal** operations than AVL trees as fewer rotations are done due to relatively relaxed balancing.

3. AVL trees store **balance factors or heights** with each node, thus requires storage for an integer per node whereas Red Black Tree requires only 1 bit of information per node.

4. Red Black Trees are used in most of the language libraries like **map, multi map, multi set** in C++ whereas AVL trees are used in **databases** where faster retrievals are required.

5.1.7. Splay Tree

Splay tree is a self-balanced BST similar to AVL tree and red and black trees. We Know the worst-case time complexity will be O(n) (in the case of skewed trees) and O(logn) in the case of

AVL trees and red and black trees which can be further reduced to $\omega(n)$ with splay trees. The average case time complexity is O(logn) only. The specialty of splay tree is that the element which is accessed recently will be splayed means moved to the root with the expectation that it will be accessed once again. If it is accessed once again then its access time will be O(1).

Most common operations performed on splay trees are insertion, deletion and search.

Search: Search operation in splay tree is similar to the search operation in any BST. The unique feature of the splay tree is whatever the element is searched that will be moved to the top or root level so that it can be accessed in a single attempt if it is accessed once again immediately.

There are three kinds of nodes in splay trees:

1. Root
2. Child of root
3. Internal node with parent and grand parent
   a) **Zig-zig case:** If it is a left child of its parent and parent is a left child of its grandparent then we perform right rotation followed a right rotation which is known as zag-zag.

      Search(x): To find the x in the splay tree we follow the same procedure, which we follow in the BST. After finding the x element in the splay tree we need to move that element to the root. To move the x into root here we need to perform a right rotation.

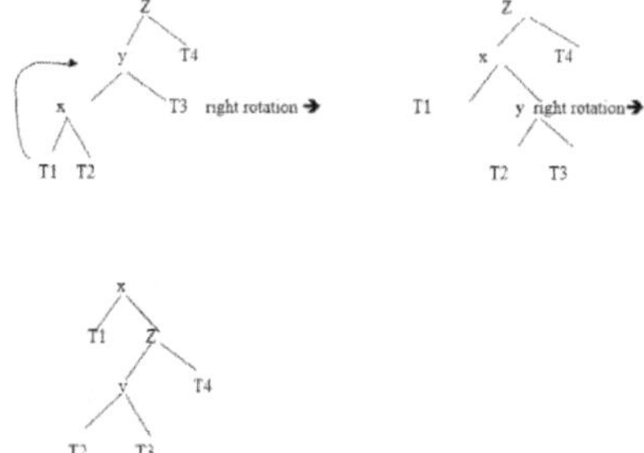

Note: T1, T2, T3 and T4 are the sub tree of the given splay tree.

   b) **Zag-zag case:** If it a right child of its parent and parent is a right child of its grandparent then we perform a left rotation followed by a left rotation which is known as zig-zig.

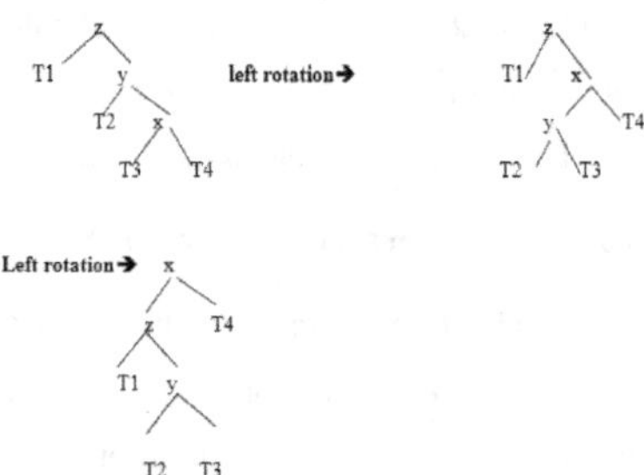

c) **Zag-zig case:** If it is a left child of its parent and parent is a right child of its grandparent then we perform right rotation followed a left rotation which is known as zag-zig.

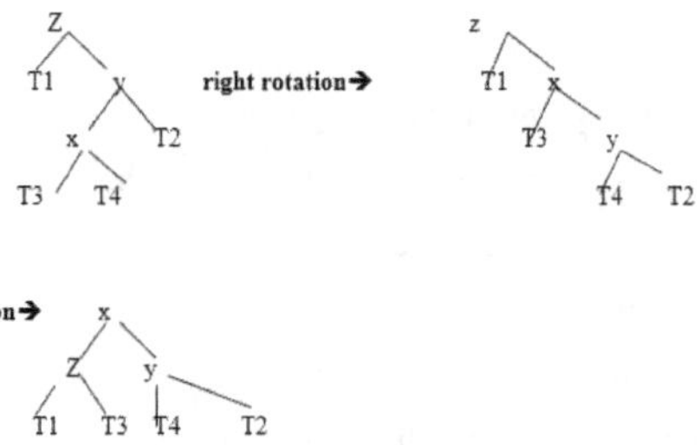

d) **Zig-zag case:** If it is a right child of its parent and parent is a left child of its grandparent then we perform left rotation followed a right rotation which is known as zig-zag.

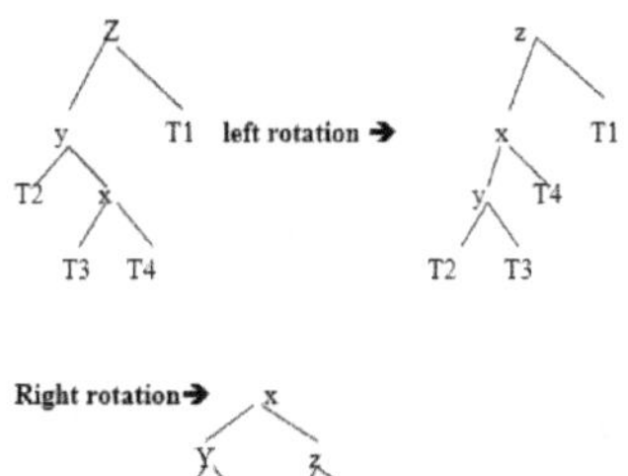

5.2. Graphs

Graphs are the nonlinear data structure, which are generally used to represent the hierarchical data or geographical data. For example, using graphs we can represent different villages and the paths between them and using this data we can find an optimal path among them. Now let us try to know what is a graph, how actually these graphs are represented, we will also discuss about different graph traversal techniques and applications of graphs also.

Definition: Graph is a set of vertices and edges. Generally, we represent a graph using G.

Then we can write G= (V, E) where V represents the set of vertices and E represents set of edges.

In a grapvertices are represented by a circle with some label inside it and edges are represented using the directed / undirected lines.

Examples:

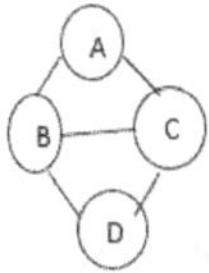

Figure 5.58: Unweighted and Undirected Graph

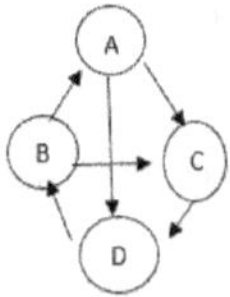

Figure 5.59: Unweighted and Directed Graph

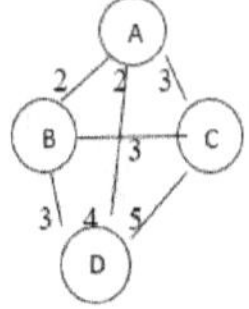

Figure 5.60: Weighted Undirected Graph

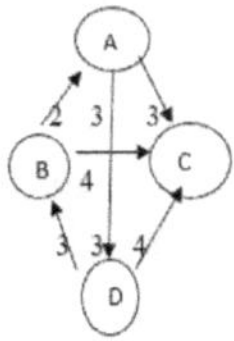

Figure 5.61: Weighted Directed Graph

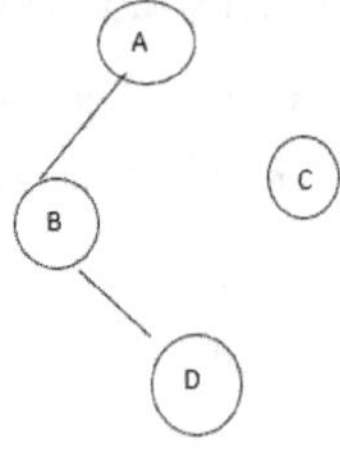

Figure 5.62: Unconnected Graph

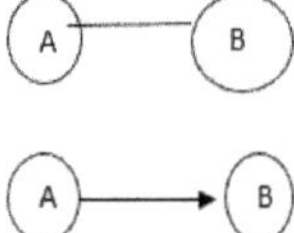

Figure 5.63: Planar Graph

Figure 5.64: Strongly Connected Graph

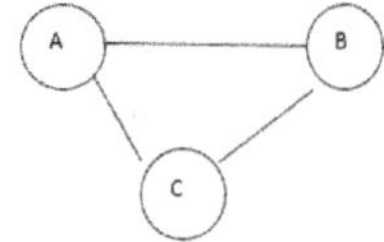

Figure 5.65: Complete Graph

Figure 5.66: Complete Graph

5.2.1. *Spanning Tree*

A spanning tree is a sub graph of the given graph G which covers all the vertices of graph G without cycle. A spanning tree is a minimally connected acyclic sub graph of the given graph G.

Ex: T1, T2 and T3 are spanning trees.

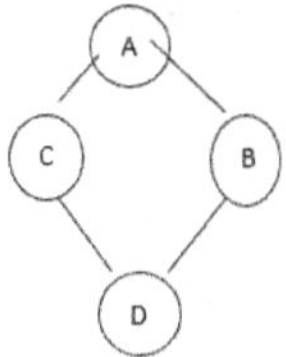

Figure 5.67: Spanning Tree T1

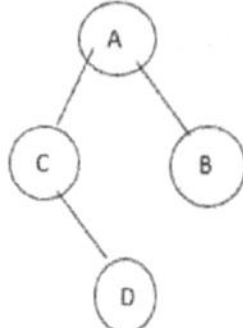

Figure 5.68: Spanning Tree T2

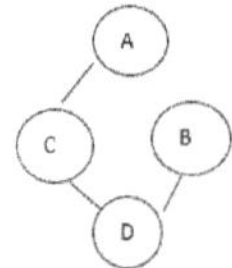

Figure 5.69: Spanning Tree T3

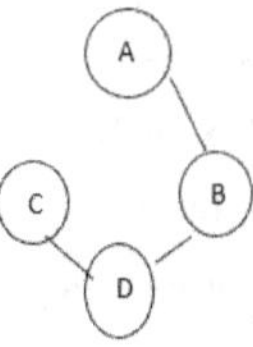

Figure 5.70: Spanning Tree T4

Note: For any graph there may be one or more than one spanning trees.

5.2.1.1. Minimal Cost Spanning Trees

A Minimal cost spanning tree is a spanning tree with minimum cost. There may be one or more than one MCST for any given graph G.

To find minimum cost spanning tree of any graph G we use algorithms like prim's and kruskal algorithms.

To show the difference between the graph G and the minimum cost spanning tree of the graph G let us the following figures.

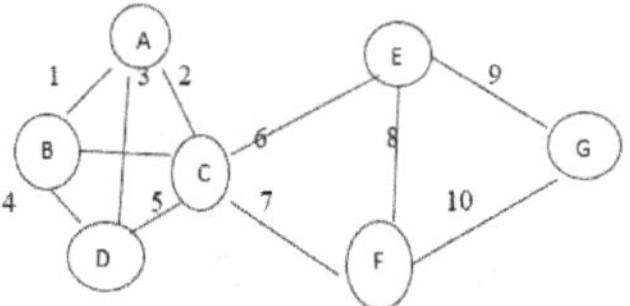

Figure 5.71: Graph G

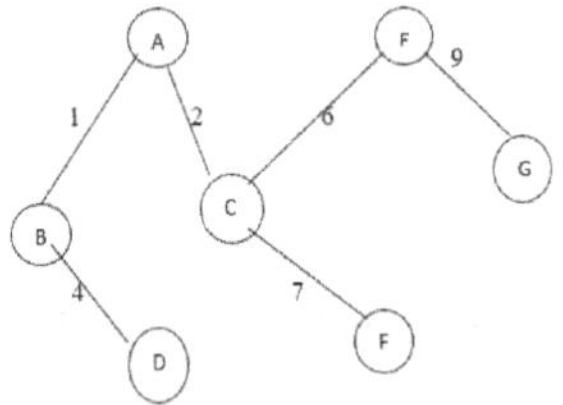

Figure 5.72: Minimal Cost Spanning Tree T

5.2.2. *Graph Traversal Techniques*

A graph traversal is nothing but visiting each and every vertex of a given graph G at least one time. Only difference between tree traversal and graph traversal is in tree traversal we visit each and every vertex only one time where as in graph traversal we may visit the vertices more than one time because in the graphs there will be cycles or loops. There are two popular graph traversal techniques known as DFS and BFS. DFS stands for depth first search traversal and BFS stands for breadth first search traversal technique. Let us try to discuss about these graphs traversal techniques one by one using some example.

1. *Depth First Search Traversal Technique (DFS)*

DFS traversal technique is similar to preorder traversal technique of a tree. In DFS we begin from the root then we visit its preorder successor then its preorder successor so on till we reach to the leaf. Mean every time we visit only the preorder successor only till we reach to the leaf level. Once after reaching to the leaf level then we move to its parent level, then we visit all the unvisited vertices at that level and proceed to its parent level and so on. Finally, we reach to the root. So in the DFS we begin our journey from the root and ends with the root only. Depth first search traversal technique uses the stack for its implementation.

Algorithm

Step 1: Visit the root, mark it as visited then add it to the stack.

Step 2: loop until the stack is empty.

Step 3: peek the stack.

Step 4: Visit the preorder successor of the root, mark it as unvisited and store in the stack.

Step 5: If a node won't have any unvisited successor then pop it from the stack.

Example: Let us consider the following graph to find the Depth first search traversal of it.

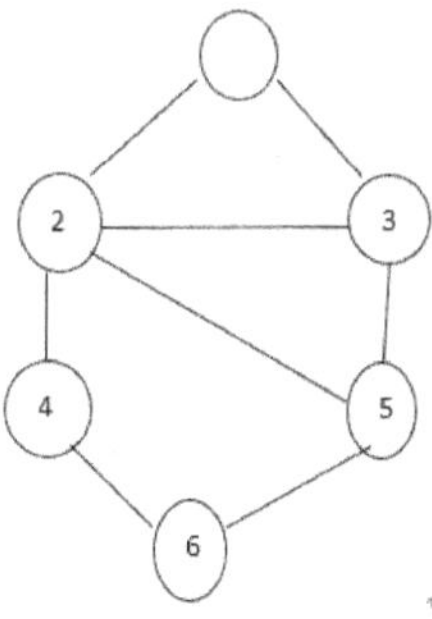

Figure 5.73: Graph GF

Sol: To find the DFS of the given graph G let us assume 1 as the starting point so we visit vertex 1 first and mark it as read. After visiting vertex 1 push the vertex 1 into the stack. Pick the preorder successor of 1 i.e. 2, mark it as read and push into the stack. Then pick the preorder successor of 2 that is 4, so visit 4 and mark it as read and push it into the stack. The vertex 4 preorder successor is 6 so visit 6 and insert into the stack. Next, we have to visit 5 where 5 is actually not the preorder successor of 6 but it is adjacent to it. After 5, next vertex to be visited is 3 because that is unvisited and adjacent to 5. After 3 is visited there are no further unvisited vertices in the graph G. As there are no unvisited vertices, we will pop the stack and we get vertex 3. Now we will cross verify once again are there any unvisited and adjacent vertices of 3 or not. As there are no adjacent and unvisited vertices for the vertex 3 we will pop the stack once again. Now we will get vertex 5, again we have to see are there any unvisited and adjacent vertices of vertex 5 or not since there are no vertices, we pop the stack once again. Now we receive vertex 6, for vertex 6 so also there are no unvisited and adjacent vertices so we pop the stack once again. Similarly, for vertices 4, 2 and 1 also there are no adjacent and unvisited vertices so we stop here. The depth first search traversal of graph G is as follows: 1, 2, 4, 6, 5 and 3.

2. *Breadth First Search Traversal Technique*

In this graph traversal technique, we visit all the vertices in the order of their birth so we call it as Breadth First Search Traversal technique. For the implementation of the BFS algorithm we generally prefer linear data structure queue. In BFS algorithm we begin from the root or the starting point by assuming it as the beginning point then we visit that vertex and mark it as visited then we proceed to the next level and visit the vertices from left to right and again move back to the next level. This process is repeated till all the vertices are visited.

Algorithm

Step 1: Visit the root or the starting vertex, mark is as visited and insert it into the queue.

Step 2: loop until the queue is empty.

Step 3: Dequeue to get the first vertex in the queue.

Step 4: Visit all the unvisited adjacent vertices of the current vertex, mark them as visited and place them in the queue.

Step 5: If there are no more unvisited adjacent vertices of the current vertex go to step2.

Example: Let us consider the following graph to find the Breadth first search traversal of it.

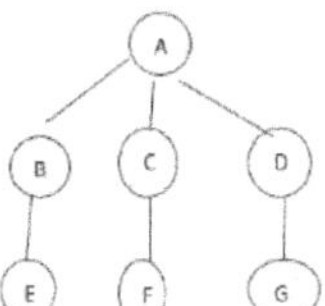

Figure 5.74: Graph G

Sol: First we have to visit vertex A because it is the root or starting and born first. Mark A, as visited, and place it in the queue. After A, next we move to the next level because at the current level there are no more unvisited vertices. So, we have move to the next level and visit all the vertices from left to right In next level the left most vertex is B so, visit B and mark it as visited and place it in the queue. At this level there are C and D vertices so we visit these vertices in order from left to right and place them in the queue. After visiting all B, C and D vertices we have to the next level, at this level we have vertices E, F and G from left to right so we visit these vertices in the same order and place them in the queue from left to right. After inserting vertex G there are no more unvisited vertices so we dequeue the queue, then we get vertex A. With vertex A there are no more unvisited and adjacent vertices so we de queue once again, now we get vertex B. For vertex B also there are no adjacent and unvisited vertices so dequeue again. Now we get C for which also there are no adjacent and unvisited vertices so we dequeue once again. Similarly, in the next time we get vertices D, E, F and G for which also there are no adjacent and unvisited vertices so we stop here. The breadth first search traversal of the above graph G is A, B, C, D, E, F and G.

Time Complexity

1. The worst-case time complexity of BFS and DFS algorithm is O (V+E) if graph is represented using linked list.
2. If the graph is represented using adjacency matrix, worst case time complexity is O (v^2).

Space Complexity

1. Breadth First Search Traversal Technique space complexity is O (V) where V represents no of vertices in the given graph G.
2. Depth First Search Traversal Technique space complexity is O (d) where d represents depth of the current path in G.

Applications of DFS Algorithm

1. DFS of an unweighted graph produces minimum cost spanning tree and all pairs shortest path tree.
2. It is used to know whether there are any cycles in the graph or not.
3. It is used to know whether the given graph G is bipartite or not.
4. To find the path between the two vertices.
5. It is used for topological sorting.

Applications of BFS Algorithm

1. It is used to find the minimum cost spanning tree and all pairs short path tree for the un weighted graphs.
2. It is used to know whether there is a loop or cycle in a graph or not.
3. It is used to know the neighbors of a given graph.
4. It is used in social networks, GPS systems, broadcasting systems and in operating systems for garbage collection.

5.3. String Matching

String matching is generally performed to know whether the given pattern string is occurring in the source string or not. String matching is also known as pattern matching. Pattern searching is an important problem in computer science. Whenever we search for some string in a word file, note pad, data base and browser the different pattern search algorithms are used. To understand what is string matching or pattern matching, let us assume that there is a string AABAAACAADAABAABA and we are looking for pattern AABA in that string. This pattern is actually present and appeared three times in the string at the starting index 0, 9 and 12. That, we can see in the below figure.

Text : A A B A A C A A D A A B A A B A

Pattern : A A B A

A A B A   A A B A

A A B A A C A A D A A B A A B A
0   1   2   3   4   5   6   7   8   9   10 11 12 13 14 15
                                         A A B A

Pattern Found at 0, 9 and 12

There are too many such algorithms for string matching. Some important such algorithms are as follows: Naïve pattern search, brute force string search, knuth-morris-pratt algorithm and Boyer Moore algorithm.

5.3.1. *Naïve Algorithm for String Matching / Pattern Searching*

Naïve algorithm is a simple easy to understand and easy implement algorithm. It does not require additional space also. It is suitable for small strings, and in this algorithm it does not require text preprocessing for pattern search. It scans the entire text only once and recognizes the pattern in the string. The worst-case time complexity is O (m * n-(m+1)) and best-case time complexity is O(n) where m represents the no of characters in the pattern and n represents the no of characters in the given string and it is assumed that n is greater than m.

Algorithm

Step 1: Read input String pattern to be searched into pat [] of size m-1.

Step 2: Read input String into str [] of size n-1 where n>m

Step 3: Call search (char* pa [], char* str [])

Step 4: Stop.

Example:

Input: txt [] = "THIS IS A TEST TEXT"

pat [] = "TEST"

Output: Pattern found at index 10

Input: txt [] = "AABAACAADAABAABA"
    Pat [] = "AABA"
Output: Pattern found at index 0
    Pattern found at index 9
    Pattern found at index 12


```cpp
// C++ program for Naive Pattern Searching algorithm
#include<bits/stdc++.h>
using namespace std;

void search(char* pat, char* txt)
{
    int M = strlen(pat);
    int N = strlen(txt);

    /* A loop to slide pat[] one by one */
    for (int i = 0; i <= N - M; i++)
    {
      int j;

      /* For current index i, check for pattern match */
      for (j = 0; j < M; j++)
        if (txt[i + j]! = pat[j])
          break;

      if (j == M) // if pat[0...M-1] = txt[i, i+1, ...i+M-1]
        cout << "Pattern found at index "   << i << endl;
    }
}
// main function
int main()
{
    char txt[] = "AABAACAADAABAAABAA";
    char pat[] = "AABA";
```

search(pat, txt);

    return 0;

}

Output:

       Pattern found at index 0

       Pattern found at index 9

       Pattern found at index 13

5.3.2. *Brute-Force String Matching*

Brute force string matching compares a given pattern with all the sub strings in the given string. This matching of a pattern with the given string will be done character by character until a mismatch is found. If a miss match is occurred they it will simply drop that substring and continues with the next substring. It uses automatic shift from mismatch to avoid unnecessary comparisons. Assume the pattern we are looking for is stored in a character array P $[0...m-1]$ where m represents the length of the pattern and the character array T $[0...n-1]$ is used to store the source string.

Algorithm

Brute_Force_String_Match(T $[0...n-1]$, $P[0...m-1]$)

for $i \leftarrow 0$ to n-m do

$j \leftarrow 0$

while $j < m$ and $P[j] = T[i+j]$ do

j ++

if $j = m$ then return i

return -1

Worst case when a shift is not made until the mth comparison, so $\Theta(nm)$.

Typically shift is made early then Average case $\Theta(n)$ or for $m \ll n$.

5.3.3. *Knuth Morris Pratt Pattern Searching Algorithm*

The naïve pattern searching algorithm doesn't work well when there are matches followed by too many mismatches. For example, consider the string "aaaaaaaaab" and assume the pattern we have to look for is "aab". KMP algorithm used degenerating property for improving the pattern search process. The worst-case time complexity is O(n) whereas the it is O(m*(n-m+1)) in naïve pattern search algorithm.

Given a text *txt [0...n-1]* and a pattern *pat [0...m-1]*, write a function *search (char pat [], char txt [])* that prints all occurrences of *pat []* in *txt []*. You may assume that *n > m*.

Examples:

> **Input:** txt[] = "THIS IS A TEST TEXT"
>
> Pat[] = "TEST"
>
> **Output**: Pattern found at index 10

> **Input**: txt[] = "AABAACAADAABAABA"
>
> Pat[] = "AABA"
>
> **Output:** Pattern found at index 0
>
> Pattern found at index 9
>
> Pattern found at index 12

The Knuth Morris Pratt pattern matching algorithm uses degenerating property (pattern having same sub-patterns appearing more than once in the pattern) of the pattern and improves the worst-case complexity to O(n). The basic idea behind KMP's algorithm is, when we notice a difference (after some matches), we already know some of the characters in the text of the next window. We take advantage of this information to avoid matching the characters that we know will anyway match. Let us consider below example to understand this.

Matching Overview

> txt = "AAAAABAAABA"
>
> pat = "AAAA"

> We contrast first window of **txt** with **pat**
>
> txt = "**AAAA**ABAAABA"
>
> pat = "**AAAA**" [Initial position]
>
> We find a match. Similar to Naïve algorithm

> In the next step, we compare next window of **txt** with **pat**.
>
> txt = "**AAAA**ABAAABA"
>
> pat = "**AAAA**" [Pattern shifted one position]

This is where KMP does optimization over Naive. In this second window, we only compare fourth A of pattern with fourth character of current window of text to decide whether current window matches or not. Since we know first three characters will anyway match, we skipped matching first three characters.

Data Preprocessing

An important question arises from the above explanation, how to know how many characters to be skipped. To know this, we pre-process pattern and prepare an integer array lps [] that tells us the count of characters to be skipped.

Overview

1. **Knuth Morris Pratt** algorithm preprocesses pat [] and constructs an auxiliary **lps []** of size m (same as size of pattern) which is used to skip characters while matching.

2. lps stands for longest proper prefix which is also suffix. A proper prefix is prefix with whole string **not** allowed. For example, prefixes of "ABC" are "", "A", "AB" and "ABC". Proper prefixes are "", "A" and "AB". Suffixes of the string are "", "C", "BC" and "ABC".

3. We search for lps in sub-patterns. More clearly, we focus on sub-strings of patterns that are either prefix or suffix.

4. For each sub-pattern pat [0...i] where i = 0 to m-1, lps[i] stores length of the maximum matching proper prefix which is also a suffix of the sub-pattern pat [0...i].

5. lps[i] = the longest proper prefix of pat [0...i]

   Which is also a suffix of pat [0...i].

Note: lps[i] could also be defined as longest prefix which is also proper suffix. We need to use properly at one place to make sure that the whole substring is not considered.

Examples of Lps[] Construction

For the pattern "AAAA",

Lps[] is [0, 1, 2, 3]

For the pattern "ABCDE",

Lps[] is [0, 0, 0, 0, 0]

For the pattern "AABAACAABAA",

lps[] is [0, 1, 0, 1, 2, 0, 1, 2, 3, 4, 5]

For the pattern "AAACAAAAAC",

lps[] is [0, 1, 2, 0, 1, 2, 3, 3, 3, 4]

For the pattern "AAABAAA",

lps[] is [0, 1, 2, 0, 1, 2, 3]

Searching Algorithm

Unlike Naive, where we slide the pattern by one and compare all characters at each shift, we use a value from lps[] to decide the next characters to be matched. The idea is to not match a character that we know will anyway match.

How to use lps [] to decide next positions (or to know a number of characters to be skipped)?

a) We start comparison of pat[j] with j = 0 with characters of current window of text.

b) We keep matching characters txt[i] and pat[j] and keep incrementing i and j while pat[j] and txt[i] keep **matching**.

c) When we see a **mismatch**.

     I) We know that characters pat [0...j-1] match with txt [i-j...i-1] (Note that j starts with 0 and increment it only when there is a match).

     II) We also know (from above definition) that lps[j-1] is count of characters of pat [0...j-1] that are both proper prefix and suffix.

     III) From above two points, we can conclude that we do not need to match these lps[j-1] characters with txt [i-j...i-1] because we know that these characters will anyway match. Let us consider above example to understand this.

Txt[] = "**AAAAABAAABA**"

Pat[] = "**AAAA**"

Lps[] = {0, 1, 2, 3}

i = 0, j = 0

txt[] = "**AAAA**ABAAABA"

pat[] = "**AAAA**"

txt[i] and pat[j] match, do i++, j++

i = 1, j = 1

txt[] = "**AAAA**ABAAABA"

pat[] = "**AAAA**"

txt[i] and pat[j] match, do i++, j++

i = 2, j = 2

txt[] = "**AAAA**ABAAABA"

pat[] = "**AAAA**"

pat[i] and pat[j] match, do i++, j++

i = 3, j = 3

txt[] = "**AAAA**ABAAABA"

pat[] = "**AAAA**"

txt[i] and pat[j] match, do i++, j++

i = 4, j = 4

Since j == M, print **pattern found** and reset j,

j = lps[j-1] = lps [3] = 3

Here unlike Naive algorithm, we do not match first three
characters of this window. Value of lps[j-1] (in above
step) gave us index of next character to match.

i = 4, j = 3

txt[] = "A**AAAA**BAAABA"

pat[] = "**AAAA**"

txt[i] and pat[j] match, do i++, j++

i = 5, j = 4

Since j == M, print **pattern found** and reset j,

j = lps[j-1] = lps[3] = 3

Again unlike Naive algorithm, we do not match first three
characters of this window. Value of lps[j-1] (in above
step) gave us index of next character to match.

i = 5, j = 3

txt[] = "AA**AAA**BAAABA"

pat[] = "**AAAA**"

txt[i] and pat[j] do NOT match and j > 0, change only j

j = lps[j-1] = lps[2] = 2

i = 5, j = 2

txt[] = "AAA**AA**BAAABA"

pat[] =   "**AAAA**"

txt[i] and pat[j] do NOT match and j > 0, change only j

j = lps[j-1] = lps[1] = 1

i = 5, j = 1

txt[] = "AAAA**ABAA**ABA"

pat[] =   "**AAAA**"

txt[i] and pat[j] do NOT match and j > 0, change only j

j = lps[j-1] = lps[0] = 0

i = 5, j = 0

txt[] = "AAAAA**BAAA**BA"

pat[] =   "**AAAA**"

txt[i] and pat[j] do NOT match and j is 0, we do i++.

i = 6, j = 0

txt[] = "AAAAAB**AAAB**A"

pat[] =   "**AAAA**"

txt[i] and pat[j] match, do i++ and j++

i = 7, j = 1

txt[] = "AAAAAB**AAAB**A"

pat[] =   "**AAAA**"

txt[i] and pat[j] match, do i++ and j++

// C++ program for implementation of KMP pattern searching algorithm

```cpp
#include <bits/stdc++.h>
 void computeLPSArray(char* pat, int M, int* lps);


// Prints occurrences of txt[] in pat[]
void KMPSearch(char* pat, char* txt)
{
   int M = strlen(pat);
   int N = strlen(txt);


   // create lps[] that will hold the longest prefix suffix values for pattern
   int lps[M];
```

```c
    // Preprocess the pattern (calculate lps[] array)
    compute LPS Array (pat, M, lps);

    int i = 0; // index for txt[]
    int j = 0; // index for pat[]
    while (i < N) {
        if (pat[j] == txt[i]) {
            j++;
            i++;
        }

        if (j == M) {
            printf("Found pattern at index %d ", i - j);
            j = lps[j - 1];
        }

        // mismatch after j matches
        else if (i < N && pat[j]! = txt[i]) {
            // Do not match lps [0...lps[j-1]] characters,
            // they will match anyway
            if (j! = 0)
                j = lps[j - 1];
            else
                i = i + 1;
        }
    }
}


// Fills lps[] for given pattern pat[0...M-1]
void computeLPSArray(char* pat, int M, int* lps)
{
    // length of the previous longest prefix suffix
```

```
    int len = 0;

    lps[0] = 0; // lps[0] is always 0

    // the loop calculates lps[i] for i = 1 to M-1
    int i = 1;
    while (i < M) {
        if (pat[i] == pat[len]) {
            len++;
            lps[i] = len;
            i++;
        }
        else // (pat[i]! = pat[len])
        {
            // This is tricky. Consider the example.
            // AAACAAAA and i = 7. The idea is similar
            // to search step.
            if (len! = 0) {
                len = lps[len - 1];

                // Also, note that we do not increment
                // i here
            }
            else // if (len == 0)
            {
                lps[i] = 0;
                i++;
            }
        }
    }
}
```

```
// Driver program to test above function
int main()
{
    char txt[] = "ABABDABACDABABCABAB";
    char pat[] = "ABABCABAB";
    KMPSearch(pat, txt);
    return 0;
}
```

Output

Found pattern at index 10.

5.3.4. Boyer Moore Algorithm for Pattern Searching

Pattern searching is an important problem in computer science. When we do search for a string in notepad/word file or browser or database, pattern searching algorithms are used to show the search results. A typical problem statement would be-Given a text txt [0...n-1] and a pattern pat [0...m-1], write a function search (char pat [], char txt []) that prints all occurrences of pat [] in txt []. You may assume that n > m.

Examples:

    Input: txt[] = "THIS IS A TEST TEXT"

           Pat[] = "TEST"

    Output: Pattern found at index 10

    Input: txt[] = "AABAACAADAABAABA"

           Pat[] = "AABA"

    Output: Pattern found at index 0

           Pattern found at index 9

           Pattern found at index 12

Text : A A B A A C A A D A A B A A B A

Pattern : A A B A

```
         A A B A                    A A B A
         A A B A A C A A D A A B A A B A
         0   1 2 3   4   5 6   7 8   9  10 11 12 13 14 15
                                          A A B A
```

Pattern Found at 1, 9 and 12

Like KMP and Finite Automata algorithms, Boyer Moore algorithm also preprocesses the pattern. Boyer Moore is a combination of following two approaches:

1) Bad Character Heuristic
2) Good Suffix Heuristic

Both of the above heuristics can also be used independently to search a pattern in a text. Let us first understand how two independent approaches work together in the Boyer Moore algorithm. If we take a look at the Naive algorithm, it slides the pattern over the text one by one. KMP algorithm does preprocessing over the pattern so that the pattern can be shifted by more than one. The Boyer Moore algorithm does preprocessing for the same reason. It processes the pattern and creates different arrays for both heuristics. At every step, it slides the pattern by the max of the slides suggested by the two heuristics. So, it uses best of the two heuristics at every step.

Unlike the previous pattern searching algorithms, Boyer Moore algorithm starts matching from the last character of the pattern.

// C++ Program for Bad Character Heuristic of Boyer Moore String Matching Algorithm

```cpp
#include <bits/stdc++.h>
using namespace std;
# define NO_OF_CHARS 256


// The preprocessing function for Boyer Moore's
// bad character heuristic
void badCharHeuristic(string str, int size,
int badchar[NO_OF_CHARS])
{
int i;

// Initialize all occurrences as -1
for (i = 0; i < NO_OF_CHARS; i++)
badchar[i] = -1;

// Fill the actual value of last occurrence
// of a character
```

```cpp
for (i = 0; i < size; i++)
badchar[(int) str[i]] = i;
}


/* A pattern searching function that uses Bad Character Heuristic of Boyer Moore Algorithm */
void search (string txt, string pat)
{
int m = pat.size();
int n = txt.size();


int badchar[NO_OF_CHARS];


/* Fill the bad character array by calling   the preprocessing function badCharHeuristic()
for given pattern */
badCharHeuristic(pat, m, bad char);


int s = 0; // s is shift of the pattern with
// respect to text
While(s <= (n - m))
{
int j = m - 1;


/* Keep reducing index j of pattern while characters of pattern and text are matching at this
shift s */
While(j >= 0 && pat[j] == txt [s + j])
j--;


/* If the pattern is present at current shift, then index j will become -1 after The above loop */
if (j < 0)
{
cout << "pattern occurs at shift = " << s << endl;
/* Shift the pattern so that the next character in text aligns with the last occurrence of it in
pattern. The condition s+m < n is necessary for the case when pattern occurs at the end
```

```cpp
   of text */
   s += (s + m < n)? m-badchar[txt [s + m]]: 1;


   }


   else
   /* Shift the pattern so that the bad character in text aligns with the last occurrence of
   it in pattern. The max function is used to make sure that we get a positive shift.
   We may get a negative shift if the last occurrence of bad character in pattern
   is on the right side of the current character. */
   s += max(1, j - badchar[txt [s + j]]);
   }
   }
   /* Driver code */
   int main()
   {
   string txt= "ABAAABCD";
   string pat = "ABC";
   search(txt, pat);
   return 0;
   }
   // This code is contributed by rathbhupendra
```

Output:

    Pattern occurs at shift = 4.